WRITE FOR YOUR LIFE

WRITE FOR YOUR LIFE

. . .

Anna Quindlen

RANDOM HOUSE

NEW YORK

Published in the United States by Random House,
an imprint and division of
Penguin Random House LLC, New York.

RANDOM HOUSE and the HOUSE colophon are
registered trademarks of Penguin Random House LLC.

Grateful acknowledgment is made to Doubleday, an imprint of the
Knopf Doubleday Publishing Group, a division of Penguin Random
House LLC, for permission to reprint an excerpt from *The Diary of a
Young Girl: The Definitive Edition* by Anne Frank, edited by
Otto H. Frank and Mirjam Pressler, translated by Susan Massotty,
translation copyright © 1995 by Penguin Random House LLC.
Used by permission of Doubleday, an imprint of the Knopf Doubleday
Publishing Group, a division of Penguin Random House LLC.

LIBRARY OF CONGRESS CATALOGING-IN-PUBLICATION DATA
NAMES: Quindlen, Anna, author.
TITLE: Write for your life / Anna Quindlen.
DESCRIPTION: New York: Random House, 2022.
IDENTIFIERS: LCCN 2021039050 (print) | LCCN 2021039051
(ebook) | ISBN 9780593229835 (hardcover) |
ISBN 9780593229842 (ebook)
SUBJECTS: LCSH: Authorship.
CLASSIFICATION: LCC PN147 .Q56 2022 (print) |
LCC PN147 (ebook) | DDC 808.02—dc23/eng/20211118
LC record available at https://lccn.loc.gov/2021039050
LC ebook record available at https://lccn.loc.gov/2021039051

Printed in the United States of America
on acid-free paper

randomhousebooks.com

2 4 6 8 9 7 5 3 1

FIRST EDITION

Title-page art from iStock

Book design by Barbara M. Bachman

For Ivy:

Nana can't wait to read

your stories

WRITE FOR YOUR LIFE

I have to write
to discover what
I am doing.

——FLANNERY O'CONNOR

Infinitive

...

ONE FRIDAY IN MID-JUNE MANY YEARS ago, a girl leapt from her bed and went into her parents' room, then downstairs. In the living room her family gathered so that she could open her presents. Thirteen. It's a birthday of moment, the first teenage year, the beginning of becoming a woman and an adult.

Perhaps as a suggestion of that becoming, she was given a brooch. Perhaps as a reflection of her role as the youngest, the child, she was given a jigsaw puzzle and some candy. But the present she liked best was given to her by her mother and father. It was a diary covered in red-and-white plaid cloth. She called it Kitty. On the first page she wrote, "I hope I shall be able to confide in you completely, as I have never been able to do in anyone before, and I hope that you will be a great support and comfort to me."

It was 1942. By 1945 the girl would be dead of typhus, murdered really, and Kitty would be on her way to becoming a kind of literary living legend.

The girl was Anne Frank, the daughter of Reform Jews living in Amsterdam. Less than a month after that birthday, Anne took Kitty with her into hiding in an attic area used for storage atop her father's business offices. "The four of us were wrapped in so many layers of clothes it looked as if we were going off to spend the night in a refrigerator," she wrote, "and all that just so we could take more clothes with us. No Jew in our situation would dare leave the house with a suitcase full of clothes."

"It's so amazing," a girl once said to me when I was speaking at a middle school book fair, "that a thirteen-year-old girl was able to write a bestselling book."

What sometimes gets lost, in the many decades since her father first published Anne Frank's diary, in the millions upon millions of copies it has sold in dozens of languages, is that when she first began, Anne Frank wasn't writing a book. She was talking to herself. And she was talking to herself in a way that any of us can do too. She was finding solace in writing her life, her thoughts and feelings, day after day. Words to live by.

Anne Frank was living through an extraordinary experience, an extraordinary time, an extraordinary horror, and to ground herself she was committing everything to paper, much of it not particularly profound. The curtains at the windows, the cupboard to hide the door. She writes about how everyone thinks she is badly behaved, about how much she hates algebra and geometry. Eventually she ran out of space in the birthday diary and continued in exercise books and accounting ledgers from the office below. In some ways she sounds like a typical teenager: a mother who doesn't understand her, a boy she wants to be alone with. In others, surely not: the toilet that cannot be flushed for the entire day, the enforced silence to forestall the unexpected footsteps on the stairs, the sound of those footsteps evoking terror because of what the family Frank has heard is happening in the world outside the attic.

But Anne's diary is also instructive about how writing, for anyone, for everyone, for you and for me, can normalize the abnormal and feed the spirit, whether during exceptional moments of history or just ordinary moments of everyday life. For those far along in the span of their lifetimes, writing offers an opportunity to look back, a message in a bottle that says, This was life. This was how it was, this was who I was. For young people like Anne, it's a way of understanding yourself, hearing your own voice, puzzling out your identity.

Journals and diaries were once a given for girls of a certain age; many a woman has cleaned out the childhood bedroom in which she once shut out the world and discovered a world within, within the pages of a forgotten book festooned with flowers or covered in fabric, written in a hand recognizable but perhaps hardened by the years. We cringe; we read. Is this really who we once were? Yes, it is.

In fact it is part of how we discovered who we once were, by writing it down for an audience of one: me, myself, and I. The revelations sidle in and slip out, the parties, the meetups and hangouts. The night of the terrible drunk. The day of the great disappointment. Or sometimes, even sadder, we must read between the lines. Some diary entries can reflect a fantasy of adolescence, filled with friends and so very much fun, when from the safe vantage point of maturity it is possible to remember too the misery, the insecurity.

There's no question that at various times we lie to ourselves when we write. I don't imagine there are many mothers who have a baby book that contains musings about unbearable fatigue or the rigors of breastfeeding or the fear of not being cut out for the job. Kierkegaard said that life must be lived forward but can only be understood backward.

Writers don't have a corner on the market of writing, although sometimes that is how it seems to feel. Centuries ago literacy, the ability to read and therefore to write, was the purview almost exclusively of the aristocracy and the clergy. But by the early twentieth century the majority of Americans could read, and many of them wrote, letters and journals and personal histories. Literacy had once been a way of keeping people in their place, poor people, enslaved people, immigrants. For centuries only the rich or highly educated could read, write, and so have a voice. When literacy was democratized, it changed everything because the voices of the few and the privileged were supplanted by a chorus of the many, from many walks of life. People used words, not simply for treatises or sacred texts but to connect with others like themselves, who might not be learned but were certainly human. Writing was a kind of hand-shake or embrace: Hello, I see you. I want to know and understand you. I want to understand myself.

That explains why Erin Gruwell did what she did at Wilson High School in Long Beach, California, a place labeled many years ago by MTV the "gangsta rap capital" of the United States. In 1994 Erin showed up at Wilson, and like many a newbie teacher she was saddled with what she was told were the hard cases, the first-year students who had learning disabilities, disciplinary issues, even juvenile records. "Unteachable" was the word that was used.

Her plans for the future, for their future, began to unfold when, as a student teacher, she intercepted a racist caricature of a boy in her class, a student who, rumor had it, had once threatened a teacher with a gun. The picture, drawn by one of his classmates, was a study in stereotypes, the features of a Black student inflated to grotesque proportions. Erin told the class that it was exactly the type of propaganda the Nazis had used during the Holocaust when they circulated caricatures of Jewish citizens. Seeing the blank stares, she asked who had heard of the Holocaust. Not a single student raised a hand. When she asked how many had been shot at, almost every hand went up.

She was young and idealistic, and she decided that one way for her students to survive, to learn, to succeed, was to see their own stories on the page. "I've always felt that when you write, you don't feel so alone, and I felt as though they needed that," she says, looking back. And so although virtually all of her students thought of themselves as not-writers, she assigned them to keep journals. "I took away everything that would have been a distraction," she recalls, "spelling, punctuation, grammar. It was reckless abandon." (In her own journal at the time she wrote, "When I ask them what a dangling modifier is, they say, 'Dangle this.' ")

Here's some of what Ms. Gruwell got from her students:

"The whole day at school, I couldn't keep my mind off my new gun. I felt like a little boy with a shining new toy."

"I am living a lie. I am struggling with a deep secret—being a 'closet drinker.' "

"I can still feel the sting from the belt on my back and legs as he violently lashed me in his usual drunken state of mind."

"Sorry, diary, I was going to try not to do it tonight, but the little baggie of white powder is calling my name."

You get the idea. The students also wrote about gang warfare, sexual assault, suicide attempts, apartment evictions, and the constant fear of being unmasked as undocumented in America, things that many think of as aberrational, or other, and which these students considered events just as everyday as Anne Frank did her Jewish family layering on clothing so they would not be seen with telltale suitcases.

Erin's students were supposed to move on to other teachers, other classes, at the end of that first year, but in a way they had stopped being an English class and become a writing community. Through a combination of the publicity that her approach garnered and the connections she made, Erin managed to stay with this group of students for four years. They called themselves the Freedom Writers, and in the same way that Kitty became a kind of friend to Anne in the attic, their journals became the confidants of kids who had a lot to talk about and no one to talk with.

Like Anne Frank, the students in room 203 at Wilson started out writing for themselves. But their aspirations changed as they wrote, and as they felt the power of writing. A group of them went to Washington, D.C., to deliver a collection of their journal entries to the secretary of education. And like Anne, who eventually began to edit her work with an eye toward publication, the Freedom Writers, with the help of their teacher, decided to have that collection published as a book. Called *The Freedom Writers Diary,* it made it to the top spot on the *New York Times* bestseller list. It became a kind of bible for teachers who wanted to use writing as Erin had, to allow their students not only to succeed in the classroom but to thrive as people. It became a kind of lighthouse for those students who thought no one would care if they wrote about their own hard times and setbacks.

The program Erin started and the students she first started it with went on even after the original Freedom Writers graduated from high school. Other kids, younger kids, kids all over the country went online to write under the Freedom Writers rubric: foster kids, homeless kids, kids living with abuse and addiction. Some wrote with pen in journals. Some wrote on laptops. Some wrote on their phones. As for the original Freedom Writers, after two decades they updated their journal entries. Some went to college, some to the military. The boy who drew the caricature that started it all grew into a man with a teenage son, a man who vows he will make certain his child is not a bully, or bullied himself.

They reflected on what those years writing in their journals had meant to them, in ways that illustrate the power and the glory that writing can hold for people who are not professional writers. "Writing in my diary helped normalize the act of writing. I was able to view it as a way of reflecting on my strengths and weaknesses, especially since I didn't really have anyone to talk to in my family." This from a student who had talked passionately about hating writing when she first landed in Ms. Gruwell's classroom. This from a woman who had just finished the dissertation for her doctorate. This from a veteran of a class that was deemed unteachable.

One day several years ago, for reasons inexplicable, I decided that what I really needed to do was assemble for each of my children a stack of the books I had written. I pulled out three tote bags—there are always plenty of tote bags in our house, but never a Phillips-head screwdriver or Scotch tape—and filled them one by one. The closet of each bedroom now had a collection of the books I'd written, and after a few days one of my kids said, "What's the deal with the books?"

The deal with the books, when I drilled down on my own motives, was that they were my last will and testament. In these pages I hoped my children would find me when I was gone. The fact is, the books are only collections of words; the motto of the nun who founded the order that educated me as a girl, Cornelia Connelly, was "Actions, not words." The fallacy in that quote is that words *are* actions. They punch, tear, hurt, harm, soothe, amuse, educate, illuminate. They express ideas and feelings, and they make people feel better, and they move them to tears, and they enrage them, and they define them. We are all made of nouns, live by verbs, enlarge and entertain ourselves with adjectives and adverbs.

"Only connect," E. M. Forster wrote in *How-ards End*.

As Anne, the Freedom Writers, and all those other people who have kept journals or diaries know, writing is a way of connecting with your-self, your deepest thoughts and feelings, particu-larly when the first seem mysterious and the second hard to fathom. It is speech, observation, and understanding put down in concrete form. Despite what the students thought when Erin Gruwell asked them to write, the fact is that ev-eryone can do it, not just those who do it as a profession. Sometimes it starts just by talking to yourself on the page, writing for an audience of one: you.

"When I write I can shake off all my cares," Anne Frank confided to Kitty. "My sorrow disappears, my spirits are revived!" But like most of us, in life, in words, that's only one feeling of many. Elsewhere there are darker times, darker stories, even moments of history, when we write about the world outside of us, when Anne writes about "the appalling stories we hear about Jews" and the "march of death."

"My students were damaged and broken," Erin Gruwell recalls. "Their lives show the power of words. Writing can allow you to write a different ending to your life."

The ending to Anne Frank's life is well known. There she is, in writing again, this time on a Nazi transport list: 309, Frank, Anneliese. She died in the Bergen-Belsen concentration camp a few weeks before it was liberated by British soldiers. She was fifteen. After the Nazis had taken everyone in the attic away, the secretary who had hidden the family found what Anne had written and locked all those pages up in her desk drawer. When Anne's father returned, the only member of his family to survive, he was given the diaries and was amazed at what his daughter had done. Although at one juncture she'd written, "I seriously doubt whether anyone will ever be interested in this drivel," she'd also begun to work on editing the diary after hearing on the radio that survivors' recollections might be published after the war.

Since Otto Frank published the diary in Holland in 1947, adult readers have hailed it as a powerful history of the Holocaust and the efforts of Jews to escape Nazi persecution and destruction, while young readers have found in its account of growing up in the smothering claustrophobia of the attic a resonant metaphor for the frustrations of adolescence. But it holds another lesson for young and old, about what writing can do. Not as a book that has sold millions of copies; that is the other ending to Anne's story. The beginning is in Kitty, those pages within a diary that a young girl intended to use as a place to connect with her feelings, to record the events of her own life in her own completely authentic voice. The message is not just that she was a Jewish girl sent to her death, a diarist who would tell the world how one family had been obliged to live because of the imagined crime of their faith. The message is that writing can offer comfort to us all.

It is one reason the diary has endured: because it shows so many of us that our voices can be heard. It was a message that the Freedom

Writers came to understand, and to embrace. Improbable as it might sound, Miep Gies, the woman who hid the Franks and rescued the diary, came to speak to their class. The students cheered as she appeared. "When she described how the Gestapo captured Anne and would not allow Miep to say goodbye, it made all of us emotional," one of the Freedom Writers wrote. "My friend who was sitting next to me was crying. Since we've been studying the Holocaust, it has made him think about all the people he knows who have been killed."

Across decades and borders, across race and religion, writing connected the kids from Long Beach, who began their time in Erin Gruwell's class with no knowledge of the Holocaust, with the girl from Amsterdam who died because of it.

"I was so mad that Anne died," one student who originally resisted the book wrote, "because as she was dying, a part of me was dying with her."

For those students, many of them held hostage by diminished expectations and family tumult, what the diary told them was that it was possible to be in a dreadful situation and find a respite from events through putting down words. "I remember back in our freshman year," one of them wrote in a graduation entry, "people still didn't understand the importance of a pen instead of a gun." The power of the pen was that instead of destroying, wounding, it created, healed. The original Freedom Writers, now decades removed from the teenagers they were in room 203, have talked to Erin Gruwell about how reading those early diary entries allows them to revisit the people they once were and consider how different are the people they have become. They were young when they wrote those entries, and now they are adults, and so they can pay forward what they wrote, and therefore what they learned. They can share that path with their own children because they took the time to record it. They can show their own children that writing offers a way to understand your heart and mind.

Words can resonate through generations for all of us. That's one reason why it's important that we embrace them. A girl keeps a diary, and someday, perhaps after she has grown old and passed on, her daughter finds it. And there is that young woman, alive again on the page. As E.T. says to Elliott at the end of the movie, putting a gnarled finger on the boy's forehead, "I'll be right here." Right here in the words, in the journal, in the diaries. At the very end of an hour talking mainly about teaching writing in schools, Elyse Eidman-Aadahl, who was serving as executive director of the National Writing Project, suddenly said, "When she got older, my mother, who was not a sentimental type at all, started to play around with poems. They weren't very good poems, but at every occasion she would write a poem and give it to us. And those are completely and utterly treasured." Her voice soft and warm and a little plaintive, she added, "Writing is the gift of your presence forever."

Think of it this way: If you could look down right now and see words on paper, from anyone on earth or anyone who has left it, who would that be? And don't you, as do I, wish that person had left such a thing behind? Doesn't that argue for doing that yourself, no matter how terrifying or impossible writing may sometimes seem? It doesn't really matter what you say. It matters that you said it.

The gift of your presence forever. Anne did not realize that that was what she was doing when she wrote in the diary called Kitty. She was writing for herself, showing us the value of doing so. The words were balm. And yet they became so powerful that they also conferred eternal life. "I want to go on living even after my death," Anne Frank wrote. Done.

Barry Jenkins, the director responsible for the movies *Moonlight* and *If Beale Street Could Talk*, spoke during an interview about his work on the film adaptation of Colson Whitehead's novel *The Underground Railroad*. He said that for one pivotal scene when the camera would be panning the faces of his actors, the direction he gave them was simple: "Show me yourselves."

That's what a journal asks of a writer. **Show me yourself.** That's what can be so intimidating about it, if you are a person who has felt the need to cover yourself up, to masquerade.

Sometimes writing can be a masquerade: a love letter, for example, or a job request. You may feel like you need to position yourself as a specific sort of person in those circumstances. But the liberating thing about a journal is that in most cases it is only for you. Why hide yourself from yourself?

Anne Frank offers invaluable guidance to anyone thinking of journal writing. Personify. Perhaps one reason Anne was able to be so open was that, from the beginning, she thought of her writing as a conversation with a friend, a friend who understood, who listened, who would never pass judgment. Kitty, she called her, but of course she was Anne's other self, perhaps even, she imagined, a more insightful or accepting self. Other journal writers report writing as though to their

mothers, perhaps long gone but always beloved, or their children, who they imagine
may someday want to hear what they have to
say, honest and unvarnished. You need not
give your journal a name, but, as Jenkins said
to the actors, the point is to reveal what lies
within. There you are.

We write to taste
life twice,
in the moment and
in retrospect.

—ANAÏS NIN

Salutation

. . .

IN 2019 A YOUNG WOMAN NAMED LIZ MAGUIRE
turned an adolescent passion into a website. It
was called Flea Market Love Letters, and it included hundreds of letters Liz had collected over
the years, beginning with those written in the
1920s by a highway patrolman in Pennsylvania
to a girlfriend who seems, in print, much less interested in him than he in her. The letter ex-
changes, which are posted online in their original
handwritten versions, are all like little stories

that way, in terms of reading both what's actually on the page and what's between the lines.

The differences between writing for yourself, in a journal or simply in observations or reminiscences, and writing a letter are obvious in the letters Liz has collected. A journal is a monologue; a letter is a conversation, and in most cases when we read old letters, even the letters that belong to us, we hear only one side of that conversation. In Flea Market Love Letters this is particularly true of my favorites, the letters Sandy writes to Harry in the immediate aftermath of World War II. Sandy is in England, Harry in the United States, and the very first paragraph of her first letter, dated February 2, 1945, sets the tone for the dozens that come in the next two years:

Hello Darling, or should I say "hello stranger" but thanks for your letter anyway Harry. You know it came as quite a surprise to me—quite frankly I didn't expect to hear from you ever again—I was about to join the thousands of other girls that were "engaged"—until their fiancés hit the US.

A letter is a particularly delightful form of personal writing, but it is also a form of writing that has been cannibalized, chloroformed, and KO'd by new methods of communication. Even before the internet came along, it was in danger of extinction with the rise of the telephone. For years the two coexisted, in part because letter writing was an unshakable tradition, in part be-

cause telephone communication was first unreli-
able, then prohibitively expensive. I am part of
the last generation who grew up when a long-
distance call was a considerable investment,
when your father would look at the phone bill
and bellow, "Who talked to someone in Pitts-
burgh?," when you would hedge your bets by
asking the operator to make a call person to person, so that if whomever you wanted was not at
home you wouldn't be charged.

But before you could say "Call me," you
could suddenly get Lima or Leningrad on the
line with ease and at no additional charge. Eventually the telephone lost its cord, so that you
could make a call lying on a beach in the Carib-
bean to someone on a T-bar at a ski resort in the
Rockies. I remember a friend, a foreign corre-
spondent, calling me from a satellite phone while

taking cover in the middle of a civil war in Chechnya to complain that he hadn't had a decent cup of coffee in days. It seemed like a miracle at the time. Now, of course, the unwieldly sat phone would be replaced by a cell the size of a business card, and he could send me pictures.

That cellphone, and its big brother the laptop computer, made the personal letter seem obsolete in many ways. Why write a letter if you can send an email? Why would anyone knit a sweater when you can buy one online, or bake a cake when you can get one from the supermarket? Why read a book if you can watch the movie? Yet people still knit, and bake, and read, perhaps because in each case there is something slow, satisfying, and personal about it. If you think of letter writing as a mechanism simply to pass along information, then letters and email are fraternal twins. But in an age when we can pass along information with the push of the send button, a letter, especially a handwritten letter, becomes something different. It is something uncommon, something that arrives and makes its recipient feel special. It may even become an artifact.

Oh, how I miss letters. They constituted a kind of occasion, the envelope with my name and address and sometimes that old chestnut "SWAK" on the flap: sealed with a kiss. I once sat on the curb at the beach house waiting for the letters to arrive from my school friends elsewhere, letters simultaneously fragile and full, light to hold but stuffed with a sense of the girls I was missing. I once waited for the letters from a British pen pal, with those beautiful stamps, the etching of the queen in profile. I don't know why I didn't keep those. I guess I always figured there would be more letters, endless letters. But there aren't. Girls like the girl I once was pass me on the street now, their phones held in front of them at arm's length, talking to someone whose miniature face is on the small screen. My grandchildren call their grandfather in Beijing from their own living room, not only hearing his voice but seeing his face on their mother's tablet device.

Letters are different today than they were when they were a necessity. In the twenty-first century I do not send a letter because I want to tell you something. I do it because I want to give you something, something personal and long-lasting. There's a reason why we always envision a cache of letters tied up with a ribbon. It's because they are a gift.

No notion quite so grand first motivated Rachel Syme when people were becalmed at home during the COVID-19 outbreak, although she will admit that inspiration first struck during a time when the sound of sirens was ubiquitous in the streets of Manhattan, when the usually crowded pavements were empty of people. She had acquired a big beige electric typewriter, maybe forty years old, and she wanted to use it. First she wrote letters to family and friends, and then, in an undoubted dovetailing of new technology and old forms, she sent up a flare to her many Twitter followers to ask who would like to be paired with a pen pal. The first week there were a thousand takers, and before long thousands more. She named the effort Penpalooza, and it became something of a letter-writing phenomenon.

"Email never feels like the way to do serious,

thoughtful writing," said Rachel, who was, unlike most of the Penpalooza participants, a professional, a writer for *The New Yorker.* "There's something about the time it takes to write a letter, send it off, wait for a reply, that feels mindful, purposeful." And because of the moment in which she was writing, there was something else: "I did feel in certain ways as though I was doing history work. I'm really excited to go back in a few years and look at the letters we wrote to relive this experience."

They will likely be letters a bit like the one I'm holding in my hand at the moment. The typewriter this letter was written on needed a new ribbon. Perhaps there were none around, or none to spare. The typist doesn't seem to mind. Her work is very nicely done, not a single error of keystroke to be found. I can tell because this letter was written before erasable bond or Wite-Out. If she faltered I would see it on the page, even though what I am holding is a copy.

So much of what is chronicled in this letter sounds as though it could be written by one of the Penpalooza correspondents: As many as ninety people die here every day. All nurses are required to work twelve hours. All the schools, churches, theaters are closed. But these are the musings not of someone grappling with the COVID-19 pandemic but of Lutiant Van Wert, a Native American woman nursing soldiers in Washington, D.C., during the 1918 influenza outbreak, never dreaming that a century later the history of tragedy would repeat itself. "When I was in the Officer's barracks, four of the officers of whom I had charge, died," she wrote to a friend still at a boarding school for

Native American students in Kansas. "Two of them were married and called for their wife nearly all the time. It was sure pitiful to see them die. I was right in the wards alone with them each time, and Oh! The first one that died sure unnerved me—I had to go to the nurses' quarters and cry it out."

When you read Lutiant's letter, and those of other young women living through that 1918 flu outbreak, it creates a connection between past and present that offers perspective. A man in Virginia named Bobby Clifton found that perspective in a cedar chest and the letters his mother, Annie, aged sixteen, sent to her brother during that same epidemic. "Norfolk is some dull now," she wrote, adding that school had had to close. Bobby Clifton told a reporter that it felt like his mother, who had died years before, deep in dementia, and who had never discussed that time with her son, was guiding him through the isolation and dislocation he was experiencing himself during the 2020 pandemic. Which obviously raises the question of our contribution: Where are the letters those of us going through a crisis today will write that our own children will find in a cedar chest? Is the computer the cedar chest of the future, and how precisely will our descendants be able to pore over the contents?

Letters have always served as the soundtrack to the epic film we call history, and it's challenging to imagine how future historians will research and write without them. It's not that I expect the old epistolary relationships to be revived in the same way in the twenty-first century, for a new generation of children to have pen pals in India or Indiana, to fill drawers with loose-leaf from another ten-year-old or airmail letters, thin as dragonfly wings. It's been too easy for my children to bounce short messages back and forth all day long, like a communications tennis match.

But I wonder about the great thinkers of our time: Will there still be the kind of collected letters that are the backbone of serious study? The letters of Karl Marx, the letters of Sylvia Plath, the letters of Churchill, Roosevelt, James Joyce, and Edith Wharton, some humdrum, some historic, some merely entertaining and revealing. I think of one set of letters that changed the American political landscape, the ones Eleanor Roosevelt found when unpacking Franklin's bag, the ones that told her that her husband and her pretty young assistant, Lucy Mercer, were in love. I wonder what ever happened to those letters. Was it Eleanor who destroyed them? Perhaps Franklin's mother, Sara, who rejected Eleanor's suggestion of a divorce because she insisted it would destroy her son's political career, burned them. Whatever those letters contained, their effect was considerable. For the marriage, a kind of death knell; for the country, an activist First Lady who conspicuously felt liberated from being a devoted helpmate. I suppose in today's world Eleanor would have found incriminating texts on Franklin's phone.

But that may be a false equivalency. Does anyone write texts or emails as substantial or as telling as what we find in the letters of the past? Isn't the very nature of e-communication to be cursory in a way that will beggar the biographer going forward? Julia Baird's book about Queen

Victoria, for example, denuded of letters, might be half its length, half its richness and texture. Julia notes in the acknowledgments that the absence of letters almost did the entire project in. "One important obstacle that was proving impossible to hurdle: I could not get access to her correspondence," she wrote of the infancy of the book. But once the governor-general of Australia, her homeland, lobbied the queen's secretary on her behalf—it really *is* who you know—Victoria came to life. "The fact that I was able to sit in the round tower of Windsor Castle and read letters Victoria and Albert wrote to each other during arguments was delicious," she says, "his stern, cool pragmatism contrasting with her heated, unrelenting passion. Let alone the letter she wrote her doctor containing instructions for her burial, which I read in the archives of her doctor's descendants in Scotland." Would such a thing show up under the rubric of victoriaregina@gmail.com? The biographer thinks not. "It's hard to fathom how historians might cope in the future," she says.

But it's not just the stories of historical figures we lose with the loss of letters, like the one in the Vatican Library in which, in that gorgeous Renaissance script, Henry VIII tries to wheedle his way into Anne Boleyn's bed, to persuade her to "give up yourself body and heart to me" on his way to one of the greatest upheavals in royal, religious, and national history. We also lose that sense of ordinary life that is so rich even as it is everyday. Some time ago my son and his wife received a letter from a longtime resident of the apartment building in which they live. It was to thank his neighbors for their attentions after the death of his wife of sixty years, but he took the opportunity to describe the history of the building.

"We were a rent controlled building fast fading into the final phases of desuetude," he said of first moving there. "Things came to a head when our new landlord, a clerk who had married the old landlord's widow, turned off the heat during one of the city's coldest winters in a century." Matters improved when a rent strike led to a tenants' cooperative, but not by much: "Our collapsing water tower so full of dead pigeons that we drew beaks and claws from the faucets each morning; a super who carried a loaded gat each time he exited his apartment, and a tenant who goaded our elevator operator to the point of beating her over the head and was jailed."

NB: It is a perfectly lovely, quite desirable

co-op building now. There is heat, and the faucets have never disgorged pigeon pieces. No one
carries a gat, short for "Gatling gun." But I
wonder: Will any resident who reads this letter
ever look at their home in quite the same way
again? The water tower, the widow. The wonder.

That was a letter to a community; most letters are letters to an individual. We lose a particular sort of human interaction and intimacy
when we lose the second sort; a personal letter is
a trust exercise, like the ones they used to do at
corporate retreats, in which you fell back knowing the group was there to catch you. Except that
with a letter you usually trust that you will be
caught by one other person. It's also an exercise
in something we rarely credit anymore, and
that's deferred gratification. We are all used

to things happening quickly, almost instanta-neously, in modern life. In writing a letter, we are often required to slow down, or we slow our-selves down to get it right, particularly if we're writing to someone important to us. There's the measured push of the pen across the paper, the sealing of the envelope, the finding of the stamp, the mailbox, and the wait.

All of that is what drew Liz Maguire to the letters she's found at flea markets, and what is so alluring about the entire correspondence be-tween Sandy and Harry online, where Liz posted it all after scanning. It takes place over months, then years, slowly, surely, in small increments. One letter recorded the locket Harry sent Sandy for Christmas, even though, it developed, he was Jewish, Sandy not. Sandy complains, as women have throughout history, that Harry does not write often enough and that she worries that he may forget her. She waits, and, as we read, so do we.

"I've had a booklet loaned to me by the girl in Bath—entitled 'Brides Guide to the U.S.A.,' " she writes. "Apparently it's what they are issuing G.I. brides and it gives you all the American terms for English words and sentences—for instance the word tramp is called 'bum' in the U.S.—well 'bum' over here isn't used in the best of circles—it's usually describing one's 'sit-me-down.' " The jargon is all old movies: She calls him "you big palooka" and feels "like a heel" about a misunderstanding. There's also a letter to Harry from Sandy's mother: "Although I say it myself, she is a splendid girl, straightforward, honest and driven, her personality has made her very popular." It's like reading a novel. What would happen? Would she go to America or would the whole thing peter out? Would they wed?

There's no letter saying she's leaving for the States, and of course none once she's arrived and can call Harry a palooka in person. But for the reader there is something better, a second group of letters, written when Sandy has returned to her homeland for the coronation of the girl queen we know as Elizabeth II. The first group of letters ends in 1947, the second begins in 1953, and there is, if not a happy ending, at least a happy middle. Sandy has returned to the UK with her two little girls, who keep asking about Dada. If she is disenchanted with her Harry, there is not the slightest sense of it, quite the contrary. "I love you so damned much I couldn't possibly stretch it anymore," she writes home to him. "Don't worry ducks—I won't go astray—have absolutely no desire to, 'saving all my love for you' toots!! You'd better watch out when I get home!!"

We can only imagine the reunion! But we can imagine it, because of what's been written down. After I finished reading those letters, I started to consider how different it would have been if the two had met during other times. If they had been separated by an ocean in the 1980s, for example, their back-and-forth would have taken place over the telephone, and all of it—her uncertainty, his religion, the locket, the difference between an American bum and a British one— would have flown off into the ether, lost to us, lost to them. A decade or two later, and it might have been a bit better: texts, perhaps longish emails. I suppose Sandy could have printed those emails out, tied them with a ribbon, and put them in a drawer, but I don't think people truly do that very often, and I surely would have missed those distinctive airmail envelopes and British stamps.

But when I was done reading those letters, I also felt something deeper and sadder than a passing meditation on how progress would have obliterated or changed them. Those two little girls asking about Dada on a trip with their mother to her home country are only a little older than I am. I wonder if they ever saw those letters. I wish they had them now. For me they are a lively personal history. But for those two little girls, now grown women, they constitute an important part of the story of their lives. I imagine they would consider them a treasure.

People to whom you could/should write letters:

- *your mother and father*
- *your sisters and brothers*
- *your best friend*
- *the teacher who changed your life*
- *the nurse who cared for you in the hospital*

All of those people would surely like to receive a long email but might more thoroughly appreciate a thoughtful reflection on what

they have meant to you, on paper, by hand.
From time to time I have both received and
sent such, and know that they can be terribly
meaningful. Sometimes we assume people
know how we feel, and then when we actually
put it down in words, we realize how grati-
tude, appreciation, and love take on a larger,
more lasting meaning when they are in concrete form. Perhaps that's the best reason to
have what sometimes seem like jerry-built
occasions—Valentine's Day, Mother's Day—
not for the sake of flowers, of restaurant
meals and breakfast in bed, but because on
those days so many of us **stop and actually
write down the words "I love you."**

In the bureau drawers of so many mothers,
of so many lovers, you can find those cards
and notes. It would be a hard-hearted person

who would throw them away. It is blessed to write a letter, and to find it years later, and to know that, amid the haste of existence, you yourself took the time to do something that meant so much.

To survive,
you must tell stories.

—UMBERTO ECO

Tense

. . .

LAURA VATER WAS ON HER OBSTETRICS rotation as a medical student during the time that she herself was pregnant, and one day, in the darkest night around 2:00 A.M., when it's possible to feel like the earth is standing still, she found herself at a bedside while a woman gave birth. The baby did not live. The experience has lived inside the doctor ever since, and took her to a place she did not expect and yet embraces.

"Everyone around me seemed so stoic," she

once recalled. "And I was driving home sobbing, just sobbing. I couldn't stop. I thought, 'I have to find an outlet for what I am experiencing or it will take a terrible toll on me.'"

That is how Dr. Vater, now an oncologist, a specialty that surely brings exceptional emotional challenges, began to write as she practiced medicine. "It was not my routine to write to publish," she says, "but to process." In a career in which lifesaving is often the goal, she believes that writing helps save her emotional life, and that it can do the same for many others, not just in her profession but in the world.

Those who provide healthcare for us, the nurses, doctors, and other workers, seem uniquely challenged to use what they might consider stolen moments to ruminate on what they've seen, learned, even wept over. Their work lives are often frantic. Their constant refrain is that there is not enough time for patient care, that the current system demands that they rush through their duties, that they are drowning in protocols and paperwork.

But there is a quietly growing sense that there are few professions in which the kind of contemplation and self-examination that writing offers and requires is more necessary. Doctors and nurses provide a template for how people in other challenging lines of work can write their way into understanding, resolution, and even peace.

Perhaps the godmother of that mixed marriage of stethoscope and pen is a doctor named Rita Charon, who founded the program in narrative medicine at Columbia University's medical school and who, as an editor of a feature called "Healing Arts" in the *Journal of General Internal Medicine,* has published Dr. Vater's work. Dr. Charon pioneered a technique called parallel charts. Third-year medical students, who are accustomed to creating the kind of hospital charts with which we are most familiar—blood pressure, physical symptoms, gender, race—are asked to do something quite different. Here is how Dr. Charon describes what she tells the students about the exercise:

> If your patient dying of prostate cancer reminds you of your grandfather, who died of that disease last summer, and each time you go into the patient's room, you weep for your grandfather, you cannot write that in the hospital chart. We will not let you. And yet it has to be written

somewhere. You write it in the Parallel Chart.

Students frequently reflect in these short writings a deep connection to the humanity of patients who might otherwise be seen as simply a collection of symptoms. One student writes of his admiration for the way a woman is facing death and his hope that he could be as brave, another of his anger at a patient whose failure to pursue treatment has compromised his own health and perhaps that of his family. One young woman wrote of standing with her team in the hospital hallway and seeing an ordinary young man walking toward her; when he winks and walks on, she wonders if she is seeing God. "I hope God comes back my way and lets me in on the secret," she wrote. "Maybe then I can know how to handle pain and sickness on a daily basis."

Early studies indicate that the students who do this strengthen their ability to connect with those they treat, and with themselves, too. In one study of those assigned to write parallel charts, more than four out of five thought it was a benefit, to their work with patients and to their own peace of mind. Laura Vater does it as a matter of course. "We need to be connected to our own humanity in order to be connected to the humanity of our patients," she says. For some in the medical profession, that happens through writing. "In my life the times that I am most myself are when I am in the middle of a paragraph," says Dr. Charon, who, not coincidentally, also has a doctorate in literature and is an expert on Henry James. "Exposed, revealed, opened up. I want to open something up in the students I see. Overall this work improves the care, and the caregiver."

Cue the skeptics. "Oh, Charon," one clinician said when I asked about narrative medicine, "the writer," in a tone of voice that made that last word sound as though it were a synonym for something utterly ridiculous. This comes as no surprise to the doctors who write. Dr. Charon says, "Every time I give a grand rounds, someone says, Rita, you may have the time to do that but I don't."

Dr. Rafael Campo has also heard that sort of thing many times before. "I would share a poem on rounds," he said, "and I could almost hear the students thinking, 'Oh my God, people told me but I couldn't believe it. He really does this.' " While traditional wisdom is that members of the medical profession are so overworked as to make any pastimes almost impossible, much less the recording of the events of their day, Dr. Campo has a differing view. He says that by being attuned to the stories of his patients' lives, he is more time efficient, that he can start further along the continuum of care because he is treating not a body but a person. "I don't need to study the chart," he says of subsequent visits. "I know who I'm seeing when I walk in the room."

There is a great tradition of doctor writers, and why not? These are people who see things the rest of us could never even imagine, might prefer not to imagine at all. They see deep inside, literally. They are often there at the two most profound passages in human existence: birth and death. And therefore there has always existed a subset who delved through words. Arthur Conan Doyle, who invented Sherlock

Holmes, was a physician. So was the poet William Carlos Williams, and Anton Chekhov, who treated poor patients and almost never got paid and wrote short stories and plays as well as anyone has ever written them. "Medicine is my lawful wife and literature my mistress," he said.

Dr. Campo, who majored in English and neuroscience in college, which sounds positively Chekhovian, insists he is simultaneously writer and physician, that both share pride of place. A poet whose collections have been nominated for many prizes, his work is more overtly medical than the work of Williams or Chekhov. One poem begins, "The ventilator's rise and fall / The ambulance's siren call." The son of Cuban immigrants, Dr. Campo insists he is bilingual, not just in English and Spanish but in verse and science.

Dr. Campo is also the poetry editor of the *Journal of the American Medical Association,* a position that I was surprised to know even existed. But not only does *JAMA* publish a poem in every issue, alongside more predictable articles on things like cholesterol and colonoscopies, it is swamped with submissions, hundreds each month, sometimes from patients, usually from healthcare providers. "It speaks to that impulse to narrate what is happening in human terms," Dr. Campo says, "a space for doctors to become whole again in their clinical work."

As a sometime patient, I find that conclusion both cheering and heartbreaking: cheering that it works, heartbreaking that it is necessary. It is a conundrum, that the better we have gotten at tackling many illnesses and conditions, the further healthcare workers have sometimes moved away from the people who have them. Transplanting hearts is an occasional miracle, but touching hearts should be done every day. Looking at a patient chart on the screen of a tablet doesn't come close to looking a person in the eye. The same technology that enables an unprecedented view inside the human body sometimes distances healthcare professionals from the spirit within that body. Or, as Dr. Campo says, "We suffer, we humans, despite whether we have an antibiotic or a vaccine. The vocabulary of suffering is not the vocabulary of science but that of human interaction, and we must learn it and use it to treat our patients properly."

Like Rita Charon, Dr. Campo believes doctors writing is good not only for patients, who will have more empathetic caregivers, but for those caregivers themselves. Burnout in the healthcare professions is now as commonly discussed as any illness or treatment. "Warmth, sympathy, and understanding may outweigh the surgeon's knife or the chemist's drug," reads one version of the Hippocratic oath, but over the years the words of that oath seem to have grown distant, and the mission less people, more paper and prescriptions. "We are trained to go numb and go on," says Dr. Vater. "We need to restore ourselves."

An older doctor once told me that when he was leading medical students on rounds, one asked afterward why he had bothered to manually take the pulse of a patient they had seen. After all, weren't all the patient's vitals reflected, perhaps better than the doctor's fingers on a wrist could ever do, on the electronic screen to one side of the bed's head?

It's important, the veteran told the neophytes,

to lay hands on the people we treat, to touch them. But of course he meant more than taking a pulse. He was warning young physicians not to lose touch with the humanity of their patients, that they were treating a person, not a condition.

There is now a critical mass of those who believe that writing can remind medical students, nurses, and doctors of that fact, and can insulate them from the worst psychological effects of the kind of night drive a pregnant Laura Vater experienced after the death she witnessed in a delivery room. The cumulative effect of the stoicism Dr. Vater observed that night might lead to an emotional plateau of self-protection but also can wind up being a kind of spiritual cancer. For decades many doctors have learned to insulate themselves by doling empathy out more sparingly than they do medication. Patients have noticed, and complained, and despaired. But the conventional wisdom has largely been that this helps doctors manage the psychological cost of the work they do. Can it be that that is as outmoded as the old Victorian routine of bleeding patients, that instead limiting human connection comes at a perilous cost to all involved? Writing can excavate the heart, lay it bare. Even if its only reader is the person who wrote it in the first place, it can promote understanding, not only of others but of our deepest selves.

For decades Linda Honan, a professor at the Yale School of Nursing, oversaw a writing contest there for which I've been a judge. And over and over I have felt, reading the essays from her students, that these are nurses whom I would surely want to have treating me if I were ill. Taking vitals, inserting an IV, considering ALS and

Alzheimer's, standing by the bedsides of patients who are dying or have tried to kill themselves: Over the years they have covered so much ground, so feelingly. I don't mean to make this sound grim. I still recall laughing out loud at the midwifery student who wrote of letting her mind wander a bit at a bedside during labor, and not feeling guilty. "Honestly, this is her first baby, and it won't come out like it's on a slip and slide," she said. The thing is, like all the others, her observations showed that she was present, which sounds like a small thing unless you've been a patient who felt that the nurses and doctors were always just stopping by on their way to somewhere and someone else, that taking your blood pressure was as good as it got, that you would be forgotten before the door had even swung shut.

But Professor Honan has always said that these writing exercises are as much for her students as for their current and future patients. "We are all too crazed," she says. "We have to stop for a minute and write." To reflect. To reconnect. She says she wants her students to remember their past, and their past mistakes, to inform how they practice once they have left school and become more experienced: "I tell them I too once had the hubris of youth and thought I'd never forget." And she also says their writing has been invaluable to her as their instructor. "Honestly," she says, "as an educator I have learned more about what works and what does not for the students by reading their stories. It beats course evaluations by a mile. But there is a big caveat—you need to create a place where they can be vulnerable and share—if not, no lessons will be unearthed."

Lessons are unearthed in the nursing contest submissions, like the one from a student called to treat a pressure wound so deep that the patient, an older man named Buddy, was in horrible pain and the young nurse could actually see bone beneath skin and muscle. "Don't faint," she says over and over to herself, and then, desperate, asks, "Hey, Buddy, would you like to hear a joke?"

After the first he says, "Another." She continues, "I tell you every joke in my repertoire, many of which are not that funny and were gleaned from Laffy Taffy wrappers," and you can almost see it, the nurse standing at the bedside, trying to distract the man. Later that night she went back, and Buddy had been moved to the ICU. The writer's valedictory is to him: "Thank you for letting me see you when you were most vulnerable," she wrote. "Every patient I see in the future will benefit from what you taught me."

That's both the beauty and the pain of writing, too, isn't it? That notion of vulnerability, and of lessons learned. But how much more threatening that kind of openness must be for those who are considered, at some level, omnipotent. "Don't faint," the young nurse tells herself, because medical professionals are not expected to react to sights and sounds that would level the rest of us. It is we patients who have turned doctors into MDeities, and while we complain about bedside manner, we also often make excuses for their remove.

Rafael Campo believes there may be a shift in

those entering the profession that may be making a real difference, in what is a slowly falling burnout rate, thank God, and a changed attitude among young students toward what they do. Overseeing an arts and humanities initiative at Harvard Medical School, he was struck by the enormous diversity of his newer students, more people of color, more women. "We do still model detached concern," he said. "That's explicitly part of medical education. But these students are more comfortable and expressive in language, even though they are rigorous in terms of science. Because their own stories are so compelling, they are beginning to understand the value of narrative in being both physician and human being."

Dr. Vater agrees. Her work first appeared in print when Rita Charon chose an essay she'd written for "Healing Arts." Her essay, "The Before and After," describes examining a woman who had been in a minor car accident and whose adult daughter is at her bedside. The two women chat about dinner and the weather and the like while the third woman, the doctor, looks at the results of a CT scan that tells her that the car accident was minor but the undiagnosed lung mass is not, that she is teetering on the precipice of telling mother and daughter something that will divide their history in two, a lovely ordinary before, a terrible mortal after. "The words feel heavy as I speak them," she wrote.

The story needed to be written. Laura Vater needed to write it. Sometimes writing is a chore, for sure, but sometimes it is an uncontrollable urge and the antidote to pain. "Writing slows me down in a chaotic world," Dr. Vater says. "It anchors me and makes me a better physician."

Parallel charts: It's not simply an assignment for medical students. It's a genius way into personal writing. On one side the data, on the other a human response to those things seen in the hospital room, felt in the hallways.

But we could do some version for ourselves if we chose. Take a look at your calendar, or your class schedule. Dates, numbers, times, and yet, for each, there is an observation, or a sentiment, behind it, whether of that specific event or course or of how you were feeling that day. **There is a story behind**

our to-do lists. Dr. Charon says that one medical student told her she found no value in writing. "When I want to think about things, I go for a five-mile run," she said. So Dr. Charon asked her, after that run, to list those things that had gone through her mind. Sure enough, those passing thoughts coalesced into a kind of unified whole.

Like a patient chart, a calendar contains useful information that is pretty bloodless. What if, instead of merely the notation of a doctor's appointment at ten, there were a few sentences, even if they were about the weather, the wait in the hard plastic chairs for the nurse, the bruise at the bend of the arm from the blood draw? What if, instead of simply English seminar M/W/F at ten, there were ruminations about the terror of facing graduation, the sadness of leaving sameness behind? Someday you will look at that class schedule, buried in the bottom of a box somewhere, and be able to see what courses you took. But will you be able to revive the feeling of who you were then? The simple, forgettable notations of every day can offer a way into writing, transforming facts into feelings.

I can't play bridge.
I don't play tennis.
All those things that
people learn, and
I admire, there hasn't
seemed time for.
But what there is
time for is looking
out the window.

—ALICE MUNRO

Dash

. . .

FOR MANY YEARS A REPORTER WORKED AT *The New York Times* named Peter Kihss. He looked a little like a lanky gnome, all glassy spectacles and pale, round face and long limbs. He was excellent at what he did, the kind of reporter who seemed to know everyone and everything, who had file drawers full of reports and releases, who could turn out a hard story in no time flat and make it look easy. He typed very fast. I was a little afraid of him, which was odd because he was so kind, although he had a temper that caught fire from time to time like a match against stone.

That's what happened the day that he was told he was going to have to start writing his stories on the computers they were installing in the newsroom. They took away the typewriters and put in big, unwieldy white monitors with faint green letters, the color and the feel of phosphorescence. Copy was lost with some regularity in their mysterious innards, but they were at the time the wave of the future, and the future had arrived. So from now on we would all type our stories into these computers, and the syncopated *click click* of our typewriters, like an alphabet tap dance, would be replaced by a fainter, more muted sound.

Except for Peter Kihss. He balked.

I don't remember exactly what was said, or who did the wheedling, but Peter wasn't the kind of person you could wheedle, and when they came to take his typewriter away, he said no. A truce was reached; his typewriter was left in place, and his copy would be typed into the computer system by one of the copy kids. A story on paper seemed real. A story that disappeared into a big box did not.

That seems like a long time ago. Now the paper itself isn't even on paper for many readers. Many more people get *The New York Times* on a computer, a tablet, or a phone than get it in the old familiar broadsheet form. I get headlines on my watch.

In the beginning, technology seemed like it would enlarge our world, and in many ways it has. It's thrilling to be able to easily access the

BBC and the newspapers of the United Kingdom or, for that matter, of Chicago and Los Angeles, or even to find a long-ago classmate by simply entering the name. But in many ways technology also seems to have narrowed a worldview for many people, serving up only stories they already believe and opinions they always agree with. They go down a rabbit hole of political persuasion or personal interest, and the actual world around them dims. It's why you can peek into a teenager's room and see a face glowing in the screen's illumination, eyes milky puddles of reflected light, and two hours later see the same scene, the same seat, the same glow. You find yourself in a chat room with the sense of being connected when, at the moment of truth, you realize that instead you are alone, nose metaphorically pressed to the glass of the computer screen, in a peculiar kind of populated solitude.

I thought about this one early morning, as fog lifted slowly from the surface of the Hudson River. An enormous flock of geese rose from the water and wheeled noisily in a circle, finally setting their plump selves down and then strutting about one of the playing fields in the park. Except for one. While the rest zigged, he zagged, back out to the water's crepey surface. I waited for him to realize his mistake, and then I realized that it was not a mistake. He stayed where he was, riding the eddies, while two dozen of his fellows brayed at one another and at the passing dogs in the sparse winter grass. He preferred being alone.

Solitude can lead to a tunnel within ourselves at the end of which is a room we didn't even know was there. Writing can help lead you to that room. There were people during the COVID-19 pandemic who, alone, marooned, in essence in solitary confinement, entered it for the first time in a long time and decided to fill it with words. Not writers by profession, who have always lived a life of quasi quarantine, who usually work in some version of pajamas apart from others, who are often professional hermits. No, many of those who started to write during the pandemic were what I would call civilians. Like bread rising in a bowl on your kitchen counter instead of in a plastic bag from the supermarket, like a scarf lengthening beneath your hands instead of pulled off a store rack and placed in a shopping bag, writing, expressively, at length, became invaluable handiwork. It allowed them to feel the real when the real was precisely what they wanted and needed.

Perhaps they thought a record of what was happening would make them feel more alive, more human, more themselves. Perhaps they suddenly remembered how a letter could seem like a profound connection to another person in a way a text or email did not. No one was buying evening dresses while they were working from home virtually, in sweatpants, but retailers reported a run on notebooks, cards, and stationery. Writing, we were told, was back!

In some fashion, of course, it had never left. There is a good argument to be made that online communication has resulted in more writing, not less, certainly more writing than took place during what I think of as the telephone

interregnum. While you have to mentally re-
create what happened on a phone call—"Did
she really say that?"—you can actually reread a
text. But much of that tech prose online felt so
spontaneous as to be slapdash, unexamined. It's
why people will often say, when reminded of an
email or an online post, that they can't really
recall writing it. Every day, unthinkingly, our
lives can slip through our fingers in a cascade of
computer code. Texts are like footprints in sand.
By evening the tide has come in, and we are left
alone.

We humans often fear being alone. Naturally
there are many quotes, from some of our greatest minds, that attempt to belie this, but each of
them has the faint odor of bucking the crowd,
and most of them contrast solitude and loneliness, with the implicit acknowledgment that we

believe the first inevitably leads to the second. The world often believes this, too, so that when you are alone, everyone may assume that is what you're stuck with, what you have instead of the company any reasonable person will seek.

But it is one thing to think that you are good at being alone when you can putter around the house for a day or two, no speech, no sound, and finally use your voice when you are at the counter of the supermarket, your first words with the faint rasp of a creaky door. It is quite another to spend months alone, housebound by fear if contagion is sweeping the country and the globe. "Our language has wisely sensed these two sides of man's being alone. It has created the word 'loneliness' to express the pain of being alone. And it has created the word 'solitude' to express the glory of being alone," the philosopher Paul

Tillich once wrote. But that second assumes the element of choice; take that out of the equation and you have what many people may feel, even in pretty places and comfortable homes.

I say that knowing that we have lived through times both personal and global when the new technologies have in many ways changed and improved our way of life. Filming arrests on phones made it possible to see, unfiltered, how some people were treated by police. Uprisings across the world seized our attention because of posts on social media. How much easier is it for the bedbound to feel part of the human race in a chat room? How much less solitary does an older person, living alone and apart, feel when friends and family can be summoned onto a computer screen?

How much would have been impossible, irretrievable, broken, during the long quarantine of the COVID-19 epidemic without technology? No matter what you think of remote learning for students, there would have been no learning at all without laptops and phones. There were endless discussions of what working from home had wrought, how challenging it was to handle a business call while a toddler tromped through the room, the dog barked, the doorbell rang. But this fact is undeniable: Had we all gone home, gone into lockdown and quarantine, forty years before, there would have been no work, no school at all. When I try to imagine what it would have looked like, that pre-internet version of the pandemic, I simply can't.

But the bottom line was that the interaction, at base, was with a machine or through a machine, and not truly directly with another human.

Writing is undoubtedly interaction with another human being, even if that human being is only yourself. When the Marquis de Sade was in prison, they punished him by taking away his pen and paper, which was the greatest punishment they could effect.

When those terminals were plunked on the desks in the *Times* newsroom, it was in the name of progress. But progress too often enters the room as a binary, the computer or the typewriter, one way or another, when it should be a both. New ways elbow the old ones into the gutter and then an early grave, even if the old ones had something to recommend them that the new ones can't entirely replicate. The streets of Beijing were once filled with people on bicycles. But as Chinese citizens moved from rural areas into the cities, more and more of them acquired cars. Before long, the bicyclists were being shouldered aside.

Cars are not a replacement for bicycles, only an alternative. Reading novels digitally doesn't mean they should not still exist in actual book form. And writing emails and short takes online does not substitute for writing letters and longer reminiscences on paper. Yet it sometimes feels as though technology is pushing that sort of writing to the perimeters as surely as the cars did the bicyclists in China.

I remember, decades ago, when the footsteps of the digital age were still faint, having someone I once knew demand to be told where the internet was, where its offices could be found. It had to have a physical location, an address, my questioner insisted, and finally I said in desperation, "The internet is like God. It's everywhere."

In the years since, that has turned out to be true, although the God equivalency is specious. If the internet is like God, then it's like the one in the Joan Osborne song: "What if God was one of us? / Just a slob like one of us." Concerned not only about news alerts and encyclopedia entries but about boots on sale, recipes for the air fryer, videos of puppies, word puzzles, and porn. Everywhere. Everything you can imagine, with no fixed address. Something about an entity that is everywhere makes it feel as if it is really nowhere at all. That may be one reason why people are so painfully confessional, or so scathingly mean, online. It's not like it's really real. Kids used to be able to leave that behind at the end of the day, to shut the bedroom door on meanness. Now the name-calling follows you home on your phone or computer. There is no safe place in a wired world.

Writing, real writing, in a journal, in letters, felt somehow like a safe place while people were isolated and anxious during the pandemic. Like the bakers and the knitters, the writers yearned for a gentler time amid the trauma of a world becalmed, dominated, stifled, by an unseen force. Many wrote about what they were seeing and feeling: the empty streets of their town, the leafy college campuses whose footpaths were devoid of feet, the childbirth with both parents panting through masks. The virtual funerals.

The frantic modern world had contained no space for such a thing, and suddenly there was nothing but. It was a different feeling from simply using the computer, just as the sound of the newsroom shifted when typewriter keys ceded pride of place to the keyboard. In his 1921 Nobel Prize acceptance speech the Norwegian diplomat Christian Lous Lange said, "Technology is a useful servant but a dangerous master." The internet revolution sent the clear message that fast is better than slow. The truth, as any cook can tell you, is that both ways are good, in different places, for different kinds of things.

—

"**D**on't get it right, get it written."
What does this mean?

Waiting for the right time may mean waiting forever. Looking for insight, or inspiration, may be in vain. Just do it. Put down a word, and then another. What is the harm? No one is looking over your shoulder, passing judgment, grading the paper. A woman once told me that her writing prompt was this sentence: I don't know what to write about. She assured me that it always led somewhere.

Insisting on getting it written, not neccessarily right, is an antidote to the internal criticism so many of us bring to the table, and not just about writing. If it won't be perfect, it is suspect. It's not simply that we cannot say we are finished until the work is the way we want it; we are afraid to even begin if we don't envision eloquence on the horizon. The urge to get it exactly right often stands between you and beginning. "Don't get it right, get it written" demands composition first, cleanup later. The paralysis of perfectionism is a terrible ailment that can seep into so much of our daily lives. In writing, what it leads to is an empty page, and an empty page is neither good nor bad. It's nothing. Honestly, if the choice is between an imperfect something and nothing—well, that's easy, isn't it? Get it written. You can get it right later.

. . . the beauty
and nobility,
the august mission
and destiny,
of human
handwriting.

—GEORGE BERNARD SHAW

Personal Pronoun

...

I T'S CHALLENGING TO DEVELOP A SENSE OF connection to one of the notorious robber barons of the nineteenth century. But I have to admit to being intrigued by John Pierpont Morgan, generally known as J.P., despite the photographic portrait by Edward Steichen that makes him look as though he would happily run you down with one of the locomotives in his railroad empire. Morgan was a leader of the Episcopal Church and a devoted yachtsman; he, or some version of him, appears as Rich Uncle Penny-bags in the Monopoly game, luxurious mustache and all. No question he was in many ways what we call a piece of work.

But he was also a great collector. A lot of those rich guys with waistcoats and watch fobs, stern and mustachioed in their oil portraits, collected things, but they were what I think of as dumb things, things that someone told them they should want, perhaps someone from England or France whose lineage and accent made those collectors feel fraudulent. Snuffboxes, epergnes. Are you familiar with the epergne? Don't worry, no need.

Morgan was different. He loved important words on the page. He collected handwritten documents and manuscripts. Of Elizabeth I of England, Voltaire, and Isaac Newton. Of

Thomas Jefferson, Abraham Lincoln, and Jane Austen. He acquired the only surviving manuscript of *Paradise Lost*. And of *A Christmas Carol*.

The tale of Ebenezer Scrooge and the three spirits who turn him from a bad man into a good man in the space of a single night may be the best-known Dickens from a popular standpoint, but it's not the best: *Bleak House* is. Still, it has become a bit of a touchstone for my children because, for as long as they can remember, *A Christmas Carol* has been read aloud on Christmas Eve in their household. I get the last chapter, so I get to be Tiny Tim and say, "God bless us, every one!" to end the reading.

The manuscript, which is in the Morgan Library in New York City, is really something else. It's not simply that Scrooge, the Cratchits, and the Fezziwigs live in it; it's that Dickens does. In heavy-handed black ink he pushes forward on unlined paper, something about his script suggesting speed, or perhaps it's just that I know he wrote the book in six weeks. It's a bit terrifying to consider that this was the only copy of the novella. A fire? A flood? A disaster.

It is humbling to see how much crossing out Dickens did, how much rewriting and cutting. It reminds you of what we will never see of the work of some modern novelists, whose revisions are sanded from the rough wood of the first draft by the overwriting on the computer. The rough wood is in this manuscript; the overwriting overwhelms. The novelist John Mortimer wrote of "the obliterations achieved by a sort of undulating scrawl, patterned like the waves on the sea." They are everywhere. Dickens wrote, and was dissatisfied with his writing, and wrote again, and expunged with a heavy hand, so that it is nearly impossible to see what was there in the first place.

I wonder: Was Dickens, already famous at the time, safeguarding the possibility that someone might think to produce, or at least study, a first imperfect draft of his work? Some writers cover their tracks, burn their letters. They're not simply writing for you, or themselves, but for posterity. They don't want readers to know how they did what they did any more than the magician wants you to know how the handkerchief became the dove. Was Dickens one such?

There it is: In looking at the handwriting, the manuscript, the crossing out, I imagine the man. And there's a simple truth. Something written by hand brings a singular human presence that the typewriter or the computer cannot confer. There's plenty of good writing done that way, but when you simply glance at the page, it could be the work of anyone. But when you've written something by hand, the only person who could have done it is you. It's unmistakable you wrote this, touched it, laid hands and eyes upon it. Something written by hand is a piece of your personality on paper. Typed words are not a fair swap for handwriting, for what is, in a way, a little relic of you. Why do we even know the name John Hancock, among all the signatories of the Declaration of Independence? Because he signed in handwriting so florid that it has become a catchphrase for signing your name.

There are still many people, even many writers, who write by hand. At the outset of his memoirs President Barack Obama described working with a yellow legal pad and a roller-ball pen. "I still like writing things out in longhand, finding that a computer gives even my roughest drafts too smooth a gloss and lends half-baked thoughts the mask of tidiness," he wrote.

Jennifer Egan, a novelist who has won the Pulitzer Prize for fiction, says she, too, writes in longhand on legal pads, "because it seems to do a much better job of unlocking my unconscious, which is where the good ideas all seem to be." Then she types it all into her computer without rewriting, makes an outline after reading it over, rewrites by hand on the hard copy, then enters the rewrites in the computer to generate a new draft. (Although, she feels obliged to add, her penmanship "is dreadful—in fact my writing is very hard for even me to read, and that seems to work in favor of the method I've described

above, because it makes the writing process literally blind.")

"I'm grateful that I learned script," she says,
"as so many kids do not today, because I wouldn't
have the flow to use this method otherwise."

The novelist Mary Gordon has a stockpile of
new notebooks that she suspects she may not
live long enough to deplete entirely. "I feel like
the rhythm of the words gets mirrored in the
movement of my hand and the speed of my
blood. And it slows me down, which is a good
thing," she says. Then she types into the computer, and completely retypes for every subsequent draft. In her case the penmanship is
excellent: "I went to Catholic school," she says
with no need for further explanation. She knows
that fewer and fewer writers work as she does,
and that the computer will leave fewer traces of

the process of revision for writers to come, and for the institutions that traditionally have stored their papers for posterity. "At some point there won't be any papers," Gordon says. "There aren't going to be any drafts. They will disappear inside the computer."

My father had a file with the word "Funeral" written by hand on the tab. It was in the file cabinet between Expenses and Gas Mileage. With some regularity he would pull it out and show it to me, usually because of amendments. The wake was deleted after he attended one that he said was like a cocktail party with a coffin as the centerpiece. The burial went out in favor of cremation and scattering at sea, despite the fact that that would leave an empty space between his two wives in the cemetery. He shrugged when I brought that up. "Things change, baby," he said.

In the last two years of his life, although he wasn't conspicuously ill, he made me take the file from the file cabinet and, as he said, "hang on to it." For the last two weeks of his life I kept it in my purse. The morning of his death I laid it next to the phone. It was a godsend, the Stations of the Cross of bereavement—funeral home, church, readings at Mass, location of repast—all spelled out so that I didn't have to think, I merely had to do. I quietly mocked it when he was alive; I clung to it when he was dead. He even wrote his own obituary. "Publish as written," it said in the margin.

That file is now in my file cabinets, but it's not between anything. It's the first thing in one particular drawer, although I no longer have any use for the phone number of the funeral home in Cedarville or the lyrics to "Danny Boy," which

I knew even without a song sheet. It's there for the simple reason that it's in my father's very strong and specific handwriting. His fingers guided the pen, made these words. Even though his ashes are long gone into the Delaware Bay, this document bespeaks his very existence. So do my mother's words in black India ink, memorialized by my sister when she had them framed between the old his-and-hers wedding portraits for my elder son and his wife. "Wedding bells," it says, "June 1951," with a little sketch of a pair of bells from the woman who wanted to be an artist. I stop and look at that tiny bit every time I pass it. Prudence Quindlen was here. She lived. There is the proof, in her own hand.

What constitutes our own hand has changed during my lifetime, and become generational. The requirement that cursive writing be taught in elementary schools was dropped in the United States in 2010. For those of us of a certain age, this is almost unthinkable. How many hours did we spend with our forearms flat on a faux-wood desktop while making loops and whorls with our pencils in the service of the Palmer method, developed by a man named Austin Palmer and relying on the muscles of the arm, not the hand or fingers, to produce uniform letters. The method was the standard for decades, and it did make for pretty penmanship. My grandmother's handwriting was as gracious as a curtsy, and every bit as stylized. If you didn't mention it, believe me, Kitty Quindlen did.

When the requirement to learn cursive was dropped, I suppose it made sense at a couple of different levels: For the technogeneration, words were generated by keyboards, not pens or pencils. And for some of their parents, there were surely unpleasant memories of endless days spent mastering the seamless curves and connections that would become an acceptable lowercase *f* or uppercase *D*.

And as cursive began to creep back in— many states reinstated the requirement in the decade after it had been dropped—it came with political undertones. Some conservative lawmakers complained that children who could not write cursive could not read it, and therefore would be unable to read the Declaration of Independence, apparently skipping over the fact that typescript versions are widely available. When lawmakers in Louisiana passed a bill requiring that cursive be taught in the schools, some shouted "America!" when it was approved, perhaps forgetting the America that made it a crime for enslaved men and women in that state to be taught to write at all.

Of course there have long been writers who did not write by hand. Nietzsche used a typewriter because his eyesight was going. Mark Twain was the first significant writer to hand in a typewritten manuscript, *Life on the Mississippi*, typed by his secretary. Henry James dictated directly to his secretary, perhaps because he may have had what we now know as carpal tunnel syndrome. His secretary swore that after his death she was still getting dictation from him, but nothing was ever published posthumously.

Still, some forms seem simply antithetical to typing. There's a famous photograph of Sylvia Plath sitting on a stone wall, with a teeny little typewriter in her lap, and it looks preposterous, like an ill-wrought prop for a magazine shoot.

Poetry needs to be written by hand, doesn't it? Rafael Campo, the doctor poet, thinks so. "That physical act is what makes a poem come alive," he says. "And unlike other writing, a poem has a physical shape, a physical dimension on the page. It does not have the block arrangement of prose." Maybe Plath used that teeny typewriter for her prose work. Her poetry is handwritten, writing that looks more like printing than cursive. The most interesting piece of it is the clean copy she made of the poem "Ariel" for fellow writer Al Alvarez. The poem is full of fury, but on the copy she made for Alvarez, at the bottom, Plath has drawn the kind of stylized little flower that young girls draw in their notebooks. It's wildly inappropriate to the material but deeply reflective of the person, a good-girl coda to a crescendo of rage. All by itself it tells a story.

Handwriting tells a story. In mystery novels threatening notes are almost always written in what is described as block print; cursive would give the game away. It is personal, identifiable. Julia Baird's biography of Queen Victoria relies heavily on letters, and she says it is not only the prose but the penmanship that spoke to her. "I could see the emphatic punctuation points, the double underlining for emphasis, the second thoughts, the loops growing larger when writing carefully, and the letters flattening, becoming less legible when she was angry," says the biographer. The queen spoke through her handwriting. The signature of Queen Elizabeth I, the brilliant, strong-minded monarch who faced plots and detractors because of her gender and the circumstances of her birth, is a remarkable tell, the z underlined with artistic curlicues, the b

crowned with a flourish, the thing ended with something almost a colophon, a hybrid of a flower and a cross. It is the signature of someone who is Someone, and who wants to put the world on notice of that fact. Across centuries it speaks.

Handwriting is also intimate. There are certain moments that cry out for the handwritten. A condolence letter, for example, surely should be put down on paper by hand, no matter how bad your penmanship. Does a love letter read the same, feel the same, mean as much if it is typed? Over the years I have replied to many letters from readers, and one of the first things they mention when I meet them is not just that I wrote back but that I wrote By Hand, as though that were both more onerous and more thoughtful. And in a way I suppose it is. Writing by hand does slow you down, as Mary Gordon notes; it has to be deliberate, each letter a tiny thought process in itself.

This is one reason why Dinah Johnson started something called the Handwritten Letter Appreciation Society. "No gadgets or devices or anything electronic or mechanical that can go wrong," she says. "There's a quietness to it, no fuss." She also says that a person's handwriting conjures them up "like nothing else does (except perhaps their favorite worn-in shoes)." That intimacy, the personality of handwriting, may explain why people will stand for hours waiting to have a book signed by the author. Even if it is almost illegible, that pen stroke is evidence that there was a moment when you were face-to-face.

Perhaps it doesn't even matter what handwriting says, as long as it exists, a physical reflection of the life of a person. When I have looked at that manuscript in the Morgan Library, I stare and think, "Charles Dickens touched this, with his pen and with his hand."

And in a completely different way, I feel that about the handwriting of those I love. I store away notes, cards, and school papers from my children not only for what they say but for the irrefutable individuality and age progression contained in the hand that wrote them. I so wish I had more of my mother than those two words in India ink, which are really printing, not her actual handwriting. If I close my eyes, I imagine I can see her handwriting. But it's not the same as having paper that her pen has touched. It's not the same.

"When I was fifteen, I didn't exactly trust the words in my mouth, and that is when I began to read Yeats to my cousin, Beatrice." That's from an interview with Yusef Komunyakaa, who won the Pulitzer Prize for poetry and whose work is informed by his service in combat in Vietnam and his childhood among churchgoing people. But as the quote suggests, his **writing is informed by reading.** All writing must be.

Reading the work of others, writing down your own thoughts and feelings: The two are joined. It doesn't mean that you read to imitate; that is never desirable, often impossible. But what you can absorb, almost unconsciously, is the way some sentences have meter and rhythm, some descriptions just leap off the page, some situations are best wrought not in broad strokes but in small details.

Sometimes reading great writing can be dispiriting. It is an unusual person who can read the work of Yeats and imagine following in those massive footsteps. But it's also pretty easy to learn from bad writing: What about this doesn't move or connect with me? Why are these words falling down a well without a sound?

It's a bit like learning to build a house, only with words. Yours might look completely different from someone else's, but you understand what it takes to make the thing stand. The poetry of Komunyakaa, a Black man born in Bogalusa, Louisiana, in 1947, and William Butler Yeats, an Irishman born in Sandymount in 1865, don't necessarily seem to share the same authorial DNA. But then you read these lines from the Irish poet imagining a disaffected Irish airman fighting for the British in World War I: "Those that I fight I do not hate / Those that I guard I do not love." And you think of the opening of Komunyakaa's poem about visiting the Vietnam Veterans Memorial: "My black face fades, / hiding inside the black granite." The thing is, writing is part of a chain. We spin words, for ourselves, a few others, or even the world, out of the past—not just our own, but those of the writers we have read and absorbed.

You must do the thing
you think you cannot do.

—ELEANOR ROOSEVELT

Object

. . .

This is my rock
Where my thoughts fly about
Like small white ships
On a black sea of doubt.

MAYBE YOU NEVER FORGET YOUR FIRST poem. Which is often a bad poem. If memory serves—and that's another reason to write, because it grounds our past in the reliable amber of contemporary observation—I wrote those words when I was in fourth grade, as part of a class assignment. Surely I had no acquaintance with any black sea of doubt.

I love poetry, but I cannot master it. Many young people embrace the form. They usually seem to think it's more soulful and dramatic than prose, but I suspect deep down they also choose it because it is shorter and therefore seems easier. That's a fallacy; in fact because it is shorter, it is much, much more difficult. You read a substandard turn of phrase in a novel or even an essay, and it can fall without making too much of a splash in an entire pondful of prose. But if you read a substandard turn of phrase in a poem, slender and specific as it is, you've read a bad poem. As the mystery writer Margaret Maron once told an audience, explaining how she had given up her early desire to be a poet, "Writing bad poetry is very easy. Writing good poetry is very hard, and I realized that I couldn't do it."

My first poem was utterly of its time and

place. It had to rhyme. The rules of good writing were stricter then. None of the poems commonly memorized in school were free verse. Wordsworth's "Daffodils" and "The Children's Hour." Poe's "The Raven." Emily Dickinson. Gerard Manley Hopkins, beloved of the nuns, who became a Catholic, then a Jesuit, and at one point burned all his poems to concentrate on God, which I can't help thinking was not what God had in mind. Edwin Arlington Robinson's "Richard Cory," with that killer last line, the equivalent of the big reveal in a movie (spoiler alert): "Went home and put a bullet through his head." Who thought that was a good poem for kids?

But what mainly boggles me about that poem of mine is the very fact of the assignment. The teacher gave us that first line, and we were to add the rest. And given how creative writing seems to be wrung out of so many students by school, the very fact that we were invited to do that seems a bit of a miracle.

There's an argument about student writing that rears its head over and over again. It's been an undercurrent in teaching for decades and comes down to the battle of process versus skills. I think of it every time I think back to that rock assignment. Obviously we were being invited to express ourselves in some creative fashion, but it wasn't an either/or situation: Let your flag fly and pay no attention to the usual rules. Still, that has often become the assumption, that punctuation and spelling would be sacrificed on the altar of imagination. Belief in that either/or was the fallacy that too often helped wreck the teaching of writing in the schools.

The battle between process and skills was thrown into high relief by the work, in the early 1970s, of an English professor named Peter Elbow. He came up with a concept called freewriting, which invited people to just let it rip, open their minds and hearts, put down words and ideas without regard to some notion of correctness. "DO KEEP YOUR HANDS MOVING," says one guide to the process. In other words, just write. The message was both soothing and inspiring: Your work may not be eloquent or even correct, but if you keep at it, you will get more comfortable, and therefore more yourself, and therefore much improved. More words, more sentences, will lead to better words, better sentences.

The idea in schools was to use freewriting to allow students to be introspective and creative without focusing much on grammar or spelling, at least at the outset. That's what Erin Gruwell did with the Freedom Writers, before they'd even become the Freedom Writers. She let them pour out their feelings without regard for skills; she figured that once they got used to writing, she could bring grammar in the side door. Given the kids she was working with, who thought of themselves as lost causes, who were not looking for the right answer because they had long ago given up on ever finding it, she assumed she had to start with process and leave skills for later. "She doesn't call me lazy or stupid," one student who was dyslexic wrote of her.

This was exactly the kind of progress that freewriting promoted and predicted. But of course it would inevitably generate a backlash, the conventionalists versus the creatives. Although it was clearly meant to be a gateway to something better—many people referred to it as prewriting—it became synonymous in some circles not with liberation on the page but with plummeting standards. Made-up spelling? Non-existent commas? Not on my watch, said some educators. Although I think we could argue that a lot of what winds up online is freewriting, given its stream of consciousness and disregard for rereading and revision.

Freewriting had one overarching goal, to lead students toward self-expression. It arose out of a sad fact: The ritualistic turning away from the written word too often begins in the classroom. A lot of adults will tell you that they concluded that they could not write long before they got their driver's licenses. So much of what school writing consisted of was hung about with drudgery. Themes. Compositions. Book reports. The names have changed from generation to generation, but they all amount to the same thing: assigned writing, to be red-penciled, graded, and maybe, on a really bad day, read aloud to the rest of the class. No imagination. No joy. No good.

During her time serving as executive director of the National Writing Project, the initiative to support writing in schools that began at Berkeley in 1974, Elyse Eidman-Aadahl watched sadly as writing, particularly long-form or creative writing, became what she called "the neglected art." Her group felt that it was making progress in the decades after it first began its work, during the heyday of freewriting, but when the Common Core standards for what should be taught in every school were adopted nationwide, they included an emphasis on argumentative and explanatory writing.

For little kids there was still some of the this-is-my-rock creativity in school, but in some ways little kids need it less. They retain a lot of the kind of imaginative and imagistic thinking that makes for good storytelling and sometimes even good writing, as anyone who has had a kindergartner deconstruct a drawing can attest: "This is a shark, and the shark is trying to eat a dog who fell in the water, but the dog is swimming away to his house. . . ." All is new for them, and since so much of writing is not bowing to same-old but instead seeing the world afresh, little kids have got a head start. All the world is metaphor and simile to them.

When the pandemic of 2020 flattened a bit and some programs for children reopened, I was concerned about how my grandson would adapt to wearing a mask to preschool every day. His easy compliance made me think again about how everything—the full moon, morning snowfall, basset hounds, dandelions, cannoli—is newly minted when you're very young. Masks? Why not? Halloween every day. What fun! A fifteen-year-old would respond in a completely different fashion: Masks? We haven't worn masks before. Conventional wisdom is that teenagers are the world's great experimenters. Parents certainly feel so, when a daughter comes home with pink hair, a son with an eyebrow piercing. But adolescents are often deeply conservative by nature. New and unexpected can be destabilizing when you're excavating your own identity.

It's the fifteen-year-old who may need to be introduced not just to that sense of discovery and wonder that may have been dulled by time and custom but to the learning space required to parse who they are and who they want to be. And one of the most powerful ways to do that can be through writing: long, descriptive paragraphs about the inner landscape, random thoughts about friends and feelings, even wretched poetry about strong emotion. Don't get me wrong: Even when school assignments made room for that kind of deep dive into self, it wasn't easy. I didn't learn in classrooms not to fear writing, since, done correctly, it may wind up being a kind of emotional striptease, the equivalent of spreading your arms wide and saying, Here I am. But what teachers and writing exercises gave me was a sense that it was possible to punch through the fear and get to some other side on which lay revelation, or perhaps resonance, or at least the end of the assignment. "We're not just talking about writing," says Eidman-Aadahl. "It's about someone caring what you're talking about, someone telling you you have something to say that's worth hearing."

But the kind of writing that has that effect isn't much in evidence in school anymore. Instead the assignment nowadays, education studies show, is most often short writing that is a slightly chestier version of a multiple-choice question. Instead of "What makes your heart sing? Be detailed and specific," what often passes for a writing assignment instead is "There were three main causes of the American Revolution. Identify and discuss them." This is writing for an audience, for sure, that audience of one who will be grading the response, not according to prose per se, unless we consider spelling and syntax, but according to The Right Answer. It's also, perhaps not coincidentally, the way most of us write now in texts or emails. The technological form lends itself to the aphoristic, the boiled down. Identify and discuss.

In creative writing, writing in which a person limns their heart or describes their history, we are rarely aphoristic, and there is no right answer. That last is a heavy lift for all, but perhaps an impossible one for students, particularly good students who may have one eye on their grade point average and for whom The Right Answer is everything. One writing instructor told me a student who was on track to be valedictorian came to her to ask about an assignment, an invitation to write about first thoughts first thing in the morning. "I don't know what you want here," the student said. "I want what you want to give me," the teacher replied.

"That's not really helpful," said the student, desperately seeking yet another A.

There are frequent complaints about the lack of skills, but not enough, I believe, about how students have lost the creative process. I can mock that first poem of mine from a safe distance of six decades, but it was the beginning of what I know now was a growing feeling in the various classrooms I inhabited that it was possible to use words to describe the world so that the world seemed plausible. The tub-thumping for what we now call STEM—science, technology, engineering, math—reflects an understanding, girded by the research, that in the past those subjects were not being adequately embraced, especially for girls and young women. I wish there were the same level of urgency about writing in schools, but the people at the National Writing Project say there simply isn't.

For one thing, many people believe that there is still plenty of writing going on in school, that in fact written work is the basis of much of what goes on in the classroom, although the facts on the ground belie it. And there's also a sense, in a technological world, that writing, particularly creative writing, is a kind of soft science, secondary to the quantitative. Parents who have rightly concluded that a college education is a pricey investment in an uncertain future may deride the prospect: "Poetry? Really? How will that help with getting a job?" Yet one survey of executives showed that, almost universally, they rated writing skills as extremely important, no matter what business they happened to be in, and they were inclined to hire English majors because of that.

Never mind the résumé: It's also the case that as young people seem to be experiencing punishing levels of depression and anxiety, writing is an unacknowledged panacea, a craft that can lead to healthier human beings. Just think if we talked about it more often like that: Writing can lead to reflection, reflection can lead to understanding, understanding can lead to happiness. The chair of the psychology department at the University of Texas once did a study in which students were asked to write about either traumatic experiences or trivial ones for fifteen minutes over several days. Those who wrote about trauma visited the school health center less often than those who hadn't, perhaps because they'd exorcised the ghosts. In fact, medical and academic journals are now filled with the benefits of what is called expressive writing on everyone from cancer patients to couples struggling with infertility.

Yet instead of fifteen minutes of writing about the worst thing that ever happened to them, many students are instead writing short takes on course materials. One extensive study of writing instruction in schools found that out of thousands of assignments, only one in five "represented extended writing of a paragraph or more; all the rest consisted of fill-in-the-blank and short-answer exercises, and copying of information directly from the teacher's presentations— activities that are best described as writing without composing." The truth is, writing without composing is stenography. Hardly the sort of work that will unearth trauma or celebrate joy or, at the very least, lead a young person to want to confide in a journal or compose a letter to a loved one.

Even when students are writing longer pieces, here's the accepted formula: intro paragraph, three body paragraphs, conclusion. I appreciate that Picasso learned to paint apples in a bowl before he was known for cubism, but I look at that rule of thumb for writing in schools and feel like my heart has unexpectedly been encased in a very small box.

My elder son, who is a fine writer and a fluent test taker, sat for what was then the SAT writing achievement test and did well. Two years later, his brother was preparing to do the same, his brother who, when asked by an exceptionally inventive English teacher to rewrite *The Iliad* in the style of a writer other than Homer, wrote "The Siliad" in the style of Dr. Seuss. The morning of the writing test, older brother said to younger, "Whatever you do, Christopher, don't try to be creative." Intro paragraph, three body paragraphs, conclusion. In other words, The Right Answer. Younger brother did well on the test by not being creative. That's just sad.

This is in no way a criticism of teachers, who I believe have the world's most challenging and most important job. They are often hamstrung now by curricular mandates, unimaginative oversight, and the constant presence of high-stakes testing. And some of them avoid long creative writing assignments because they are skeptical about their own writing skills. Often the education curricula used to train aspiring teachers contain little about teaching creative writing, and many teachers haven't found their own way to expressing themselves on the page.

Even those teachers who assign longer essay pieces or short stories may be faced with pointing students toward revision, and when a paper is returned to a student, marked up and in need of further work, it is axiomatic that students will see what they have done as flawed. I can certainly relate. I have some fellow writer friends who love to revise. It is in the rewriting, they like to say, that the true shape of their work emerges. It is the most rewarding, even pleasurable part of the process. I learned long ago when they said this to arrange my face, because it did not seem useful to let them see my thoughts writ large there, which were basically, in some version of freewriting: ARE YOU CRAZY IT'S THE WORST I WOULD RATHER DO ANY-

THING THAN REVISE PLEASE GOD LET
MY EDITOR THINK MY FIRST DRAFT IS
FINE.

Those capital letters are no exaggeration.
Which raises the obvious question: Why comply? Because the truth is that work that has been
edited and then revised is, in my experience, no-
tably better than work that has not. But the
problem for students, particularly students who
are used to doing well, is that having a paper
handed back for another go-round implies not a
desire for improvement but a verdict of failure.
There is something wrong. The problem for
the teacher is that that's not necessarily what
she is saying. Looking at an essay is different
from grading an algebra test. Either the numbers are correct, or they are not. With an essay
it's sometimes like seeing a photograph that is

slightly out of focus. The picture is compelling, if only it were sharper.

Not long ago I read an interview with a teacher who had come up with an interesting way of approaching revision. She'd labeled student work either publishable or revisable. In other words, it was either something good, or something moving in that direction. So much of editing feels like harsh judgment. This was promise. That, I realized, is why I open the envelope containing my editor's voluminous notes on—let's face it—what's lacking in the manuscript I've handed in. It's because there is a promise implicit in those notes, the promise of something better, perhaps even really good.

I feel so strongly about teaching creative writing in schools for one simple reason: I am a writer because of teachers. When I was in eighth grade, a very erudite nun named Mother Mary Ephrem looked up from one of my papers and said, "You are a writer." I am a writer because, time and again, I handed in a paper and was told that it was good—publishable, by the standards of that one inventive educator. But I often think that it could have gone another way, that I might have had teachers who were not much interested in written work, or who assigned the writing equivalent of an algebra test: Describe three characters in *David Copperfield*. Instead I had my rock, my small white ships on a black sea of doubt. Instead I had Miss Ritzenthaler, my senior-year English teacher, looking up from under her brows, holding in her hands an essay I had produced the night before in a haphazard fashion somewhere between talking on the phone and laying out a page of the student newspaper.

"This is so disappointing," she said quietly, handing it back, and she said no more. There were no red pencil marks, no grade; it was not even worthy of correction. Not even revisable. My memory is imprecise, but I can hear Miss Ritz saying that sentence as though she were sitting beside me now, and remember knowing as she said those words that I never wanted to hear them, or feel them, again.

There are many aphorisms about writing. "Write what you know" is one, although it often seems as though people write to figure out, or to test, what they know. "Show, don't tell" is another, suggesting, for instance, that instead of saying someone is beautiful you describe them so that the reader can draw their own conclusion.

The thing is, both of these rules are often overridden to good effect. Science fiction writers write about things they couldn't possibly know but improbably, and perfectly, dream up. There's a fair amount of telling in the novels of Toni Morrison and Jane Austen, but it would be hard to argue that their stories would be better without it, given the wisdom of one and the wit of the other.

With that in mind, here is the rule about when and where to write: There is none. You may have read about an admired writer who swears by sitting down at the desk before the sun is up, and thought, "Well, I'm not an early bird, I'm sunk." You may have heard about a successful writer who finished a book loitering at a diner table, and thought, "Well, I can't deal with distractions. That's that."

That's not that. Writing habits are as idio-syncratic as eating habits, or speaking syntax, or hairstyle, or clothes. Some people like to open their journals first thing in the morning, to reflect on the day before and consider the day ahead, and some people like to prop them on their knees in bed before turning off the light. Some can write anywhere, on subway trains, in coffee shops. Others need that specific spot, the desk, the bench.

The memoirs of writers, the behavior of friends, make clear that time and place for writing is like anything else, like whether you're an early-to-bed person or a night owl: It is highly individual. So don't make how it's done an excuse. **How it's done is how you do it.** If day-break is a time for strong coffee and muddled thinking, then perhaps your moment is after dinner. If the evening is when you let your brain marinate after the demands of the day, there's always lunchtime. You can eat with one hand and write with the other. I know. There are mayonnaise stains on some of my notes.

There is no agony
like bearing an untold
story inside you.

—ZORA NEALE HURSTON

Conjugate

...

THERE IS A WOMAN IN MY NEW YORK CITY neighborhood who is blind and who walks accompanied by a guide dog, a yellow Labrador. I am in awe of them, the woman and dog both, because they easily traverse the streets of Manhattan, which are confounding enough for anyone: noisy, crowded, rife with obstacles. A wire trash can overflowing on one corner, a crew excavating a water main on another, a little girl on a scooter going pell-mell with her father in pursuit. I bob and weave and zig and zag because I can see what's coming. What it's like not to be able to do so is incomprehensible to me, although I can imagine that those people who are blind get terribly weary of hearing sighted people like me say that.

The woman in my neighborhood is clearly completely competent. Without the unmistakable leather U harness, you would think she was just someone out walking her dog, which of course she is. I have two Labradors, and I have to pick up after them when they go to the bathroom in the street. Maybe guide dogs, remarkable as they seem, have been trained to go in some unobtrusive corner of the gutter.

One morning, woman and dog came down the street as usual, heading toward a rectangle of yellow hazard tape put there to block an area being repaved. The tape was set high enough that the dog could pass beneath and through, and the dog did. But the woman hit the tape, and stopped.

I was right behind her, and I paused, because her utter confidence made me wonder if she would see an offer of assistance as condescending. I was paralyzed by the possibility of giving offense. But at least, I thought, I could explain the mistake the dog had made, and I did. I offered my arm, and she grasped it lightly, and we tentatively took to the street to get around the area of pavement. Then my neighbor and her dog walked on. And for a few minutes it was nothing but an interior anecdote, passing eventually, as these things do, into memory.

But written down, it lives. It's there, it's real. That's the important thing. That's why we write things down, to give them life. Sometimes people ask whether a particularly difficult or challenging situation is made cathartic through writing. I'm not sure writing about things always makes us feel better, but perhaps it sometimes does make loss, tragedies, disappointments more actual. It can turn them into something with a clearer shape and form, and therefore make it possible to see them more deeply and clearly, and more usefully turn confusion and pain into understanding and perhaps reconciliation. On paper our greatest challenges become A Real Thing, in a world in which so much seems ephemeral and transitory.

That is a kind of afterlife all our own stories, inconsequential and important as well, can assume when we record them. To write the present is to believe in the future. One of the poignant things about Anne Frank's diary is that the very act of composition suggests that someday she will live to tell it all, and in some sense I suppose she does, on the page, in the attic, surviving day by day, never dreaming that by doing so she will help some of us survive, too. She's not really writing the story of the Holocaust, although that's what she illuminates. She's telling the story of one small and unremarkable life that has come to stand for millions of others, and so became remarkable.

So what if your story of a small, unremarkable life is read only by you, in some quiet corner, or by one or two people you love and trust to understand? If those are people who can learn from and value it, isn't that a notable achievement, a valuable audience? Audience is, after all, one of the great barriers to writing, those outsiders who will peek in and sadly shake their heads: oh, no, not good enough. Even after all this time I still fear that judgment.

The wonderful thing about a journal, or a personal letter, is that most of the time there is no need to fear the audience. Someday that audience may grow, if the journal is passed down through generations, and the letters, too. But for now the face of the reader is a friendly face, seen either in the mirror or across an imagined table.

Sometimes people will tell me something I wrote made them feel less alone. But the fact is, I feel less alone when I write as well. The process models a kind of empathy, because even if you are simply writing your own experiences, your own feelings, it assumes an ability to connect on a human level, to meet some unspoken need of your own, and maybe of someone else's, too. One of the Freedom Writers, who was homeless as a child and has written about the feelings of despair and shame, wrote ten years out of school about sharing his work with others: "Every time I tell my story, I reopen the wound and relive my childhood. What helps me persevere isn't the pity people feel for me, or the praise and congratulations at the end. It is when I look into the audience and recognize the familiar pain in someone's face as he or she connects to my story." So true, what he says: The process is not always easy, but the result is sometimes invaluable.

The difficulty of that process can drive people away from writing, convince them that they cannot, should not, write because they find it arduous. Somehow we have come to believe that if we are good at something it will not be difficult, that there will not be false starts, bad results, frustration, anguish. A natural, people say admiringly, and what they mean is hard things done with seeming ease, and therefore apparently without effort. I'm not sure why anyone believes this, because the notion is absurd, and not just in writing. A surgeon becomes a great surgeon by years of concentrated effort, attention, repetition. An Olympic medalist does the same routine over and over and over again. The cookbook doyenne Ina Garten, who is considered the queen of the simple, luscious meal, has a catchphrase: "How easy is that?" But in an interview she once said, "I find cooking hard." She tests recipes many times, and then has assistants test them as well. It can be easy for you because it was laborious for her.

"Writing is easy. You just sit down at the

typewriter and open a vein." I've heard that over and over again, although no one seems to know for sure who said it. For years I ascribed it to Dorothy Parker, the fabled wit, but then someone told me the quote actually came from Red Smith, the legendary sportswriter. It's not Oscar Wilde, who seems to have been the source for many memorable observations, and it's clearly not Shakespeare, who has more turns of phrase to his credit than anyone except perhaps the Bible.

(Another excellent quote that seems to have questionable provenance is this one: "Eternity is two people and a ham." Dorothy Parker gets tagged with that, too, but I've also seen it claimed for Irma Rombauer, who wrote *The Joy of Cooking*, and, of all people, Abraham Lincoln. One day I asked the writer Calvin Trillin if he knew who said it. "No," he replied, "who was it?" "No one is sure," I said. "Oh," he said, "it was me. From now on just tell people it was me.")

Here's the thing about the ham quote (said by Calvin Trillin): It's really accurate. Here's the thing about the writing quote: It's really great, and to me it feels really wrong. Many people don't find writing easy, and it's certainly not as simple as opening a vein. I know what whoever said that meant, of course. Some writing pours out of you in a flood of strong emotion, out of love, or fear, or anger, or passion. Some writing is bloody because it is visceral. But much is not. Some of the journal entries of Anne Frank and of the Freedom Writers are about love and loss, life and death, and some are ephemera and everyday arrangements. You shouldn't feel put off if you are writing about small, not monumental events. Sometimes that's the way it works.

But another problem with the adage about opening a vein is that the way it is phrased suggests that while writing is painful, it is also somehow reflexive, that the words will just erupt in a stream of feeling. So if people can't find the vein, they abandon the effort. The entire thing contributes to a kind of fantastical, fairy-tale view of composition, of sitting down and spewing words, sentences, paragraphs in a welter of emotion, cousin to the composer with his hair standing on end as he hammers away at the piano in a fit of creative possession. Sometimes, maybe. But most of the writers I know, and many long gone whom I've read about, did not find writing easy. There are exceptions, of course. Dickens, who worked at a standing desk, sometimes wrote while parties were going on around him. Although Edith Wharton described herself as a slow worker, she must have been a somewhat facile one. She wrote in longhand in bed each morning, dropping sheets of stationery one by one to be gathered and typed by what must have been an exceptionally literary secretary. Like most writers, many of whom eat the same meal and keep to the same schedule every day, Wharton insisted on those mornings. As she wrote in a 1905 letter, "The slightest interruption in the household routine completely de-rails me."

When you write for a living and go out into the world and talk about it, one of the most omnipresent questions is "Where do you get your ideas?" I don't know about the rest of my colleagues, but I cook something up when I have to answer that question. It's not exactly a lie, but it's not exactly the truth either, because for a fiction writer the question of where things come from is, in my experience, a bit mysterious. Or, as the novelist E. L. Doctorow said once when I told him I was going out on a book tour, "Oh, now you will have to pretend you know how we do what we do."

The problem with leaving the issue as a bit of a mystery is that it smells of inspiration, or the muse, that sudden stroke that is meant to leave you gobsmacked for a moment at the desk and then pushing words around helter-skelter as quickly as possible, the light bulb of a dozen Looney Tunes cartoons having appeared above. It's that vein opening again, and it doesn't happen often. Madeleine L'Engle, who wrote *A Wrinkle in Time*, once said, "Inspiration usually comes during work, rather than before it." Or there's this observation, most often credited to W. Somerset Maugham: "There are three rules for writing a novel. Unfortunately no one knows what they are."

Butt in chair. That's the piece of direction I give to anyone and everyone who wants to write, who is thinking about writing, who is asking how it's done, who is fearful of and intimidated by the act. It's not poetic, and it doesn't bespeak inspiration. What it does suggest is a way into what is not a mystery but a process, a way into the story of yourself.

Butt in chair, paper and pen at hand, or computer, or typewriter. A word, then another, then another after that. "A word after a word / after a word is power," Margaret Atwood once wrote. It's like building a wall, brick by brick, and at the end you have something, but it doesn't have to be something that considers the sweeping, the notable, the historic. It doesn't have to be an account of a birth or a death or a crisis between the two.

When a young nurse named Lutiant Van Wert wrote a letter to a friend while taking care of patients during the deadly flu epidemic of 1918, she certainly talked of death and disease. But she also included a description of how, standing in line at the station, she mistakenly managed to switch bags with a soldier taking the same train to Washington, because the suitcases were so similar. "He is a perfect gentleman, and sure treated me nice on the way," she wrote.

One of the essays written for the writing contest held each year as part of the Yale School of Nursing program is entitled "How to Give a Bed Bath." What task could be more ordinary?

And yet the midwifery student who wrote it not only tells the reader exactly what the process entails, but goes on to consider the ways in which running a damp washcloth over the body of a stranger requires you to try to feel connected to that person. The ordinary stories are sometimes the most illuminating of our lives because the simply factual can lead us to the deeply philosophical. They allow us to stop time, to preserve not only who we are but who we once were.

When you write, you connect with yourself, past, present, and future. I remember myself, the little girl who once wrote poems, the college applicant who said without guile or humility that her goal in life was to be a writer. Writing can make memory concrete, and memory is such a hard thing to hold on to, like a Jell-O mold, all wiggly but with solid bits embedded clearly.

When my family was all gathered together during the endless months of COVID-19 quarantine, my daughter-in-law created an aquarium for her children, borrowing a tank from a neighbor whose boys had outgrown that kind of thing, and as the weeks went by, we all watched its contents grow. Tadpoles. Salamanders. A small fish that research told us was an eastern blacknose dace. The tadpoles turned into frogs and toads and were released. The salamanders and the fish went back into the pond. In a huge glass urn next to the aquarium we put caterpillars, and stalks of fennel to sustain them, and watched as the caterpillars wound themselves into dun-colored cocoon coats and then crawled out, their wings first damp and limp, then unfurled so they could fly away, beautiful tiger swallowtails. Sometimes it occurred to me that we were our own aquarium, our own glass jar, a small contained space set up to seem like the world, from which some-day we too would be liberated.

My grandchildren were very young when this happened. Maybe writing it down will help them remember it all. "Life is all memory," wrote Tennessee Williams, who in *The Glass Menagerie* wrote one of the great memory plays, "except for the one present moment that goes by so quick you hardly catch it going." The point is that writing is a net, catching memory and pin-ning it to the board like people sometimes do with butterflies like the ones we hatched. Writ-ing is a hedge against forgetting, forgetting for-ever.

A young woman wrote an essay in *The New York Times* about her father, who had gone down the deep mental well of Alzheimer's. She found

comfort in the old journals he had written, which
showed his brio, his zest for life, his love for his
wife and his daughter. The person he had once
been was alive in those pages. What a gift he had
left behind for those he loved! As I read that
essay, I wept, not simply because of what she
had lost—the journals just stop one day, and
never resume—but for what I had never had.

There are no journals written by my father.
If I could go back in time, I would ask him to
keep one, but maybe, like so many busy people,
he would think it was a waste of the scant hours
in his day. Why? he would ask. What would I
write about? I would offer you the same answer
I would have given him: Nothing. Everything.
He could have written a recollection of college
days gone by, or an account of the morning's
fishing getting skunked out by the secret spot, a

paragraph about the night he went out with my mother for the first time, or how he met his best friend, Ed. That's all. I wouldn't ask for the hard stuff, the bad stuff, the truth about how weighed down my father may have felt by five children in ten years, the months he spent knowing that his wife was dying and keeping that knowledge from her. I wouldn't care about revelation. I'd just like a little piece of something. That's all I want, just a little piece. Couldn't you manage that, for someone you love, who would probably treasure it every bit as much as I would?

Voice. Think of the word. The challenge for so many of us is that, in writing, at least, it stands like an unfamiliar thing, apart. Instead of honoring our own voice, the one that is so individual and specific, we think of writing in terms of other people's work. The great novels, or the beloved young-adult book. The history text, or the legal papers. The clever lyrics of a favorite song or the popular online postings. People constantly make the mistake of thinking that their words on the page should be the equivalent of dress-up clothes. Completely different from everyday. A little stiff, a little remote, proper, mannered, a world away from the T-shirt of ordinary talk.

Naturally words on the page may well be sharper, clearer, more specific than idle phone conversation or dinner table ramblings. The syntax may be cleaned up, the images made more resonant. But on the other hand, words on the page, certainly in a journal entry, usually in a letter, should carry the stamp of individuality. There are writers about whom people can say: Even if her name was not on it, I would know she wrote it. Not everyone can have a voice that distinctive, but **everyone has a voice.** Reading your words aloud after you've written them is a powerful way to make this clear. I always do it, discover that a sentence is far too long by not being able to breathe through it, hear the almost audible clunk of what looked on the page like a braid of language but to the critical ear is clearly a snarl and a knot.

If you've gone wrong, tried in print to be something you are not in life, the phrases feel like marbles in your mouth. But if you've gotten your own voice down on the page, you will read aloud and think: "Yep, that's it. That's me."

In all my life,
I have never been free.
I have never been
able to do anything
with freedom,
except in the field
of my writing.

—LANGSTON HUGHES

Past Perfect

...

IT IS A SAD AND UNDENIABLE FACT THAT history comes to us too often drained of blood and embalmed, a panoply of stiff set pieces starring great men, an array of nations and dates and documents. In classrooms, in seminars, in books, it is too often something to memorize and too seldom something to feel a part of. The distinguished historian Arthur Schlesinger, Jr., once wrote, "History is lived in the main by the unknown and forgotten. But historians perforce concentrate on the happy few who leave records, give speeches, write books, make fortunes, hold offices, win or lose battles and thrones."

In the past those happy few wrote the story, turning history into an enormous, grand house, a little like the White House, chandeliers and columns and porticoes. But where is the furniture? We are the furniture. The history people need, to understand where we have come from, what to decry and what to prize, is not a history of presidents or generals. It is the history of us, and one reason ordinary people must write is to leave their own records, to furnish the rooms of our country and our world.

We know this from experience. We have grown up with history right before our eyes. Some of us had grandparents who soldiered through the flu epidemic of 1918, the Great Depression, two world wars within memory of each other, the first called the Great War until one day it turned out it had been eclipsed by another. Everything they'd lived through marked them. When my grandfather insisted I eat the stringy white stuff clinging to an orange like a shroud, my father would say he had a Depression mentality. My grandmother never ate candy because she had offered it up to the Lord in exchange for the safe return of her son Francis, who was a POW during World War II. My father could still remember what pew his family occupied at Most Blessed Sacrament on the Sunday Harry Truman said that the war was over, and how his mother stayed in church, her rosary looped around her hand, the crucifix dangling. In school what I learned about World War II was Pearl Harbor, D-Day, the British blitz, the death camps. All those things are important. But to feel the centuries deep in our bones, it is also important to know the small moments, the human moments, the pew, the rosary.

To the extent that our knowledge of history is enlarged by those small moments, they often come not in writing but in stories told at our kitchen tables, at family reunions, over beers in the backyard. There's unquestionably value to that oral tradition, but it's suspect, too. You've surely listened as the stories of your own family, once told, became bigger, broader, more color- ful, blown up like a balloon until they'd lost some of the shape of real life. I wonder, if they'd been written down by those intimately involved, whether they might have been different, maybe more authentic. Oral accounts are always medi- ated by teller and by time.

The morphing of individual history when it is spoken to others and not personally written has certainly occurred to scholars considering the "Slave Narratives" generated as part of the Works Progress Administration in the 1930s. An attempt to interview more than two thousand people who had been enslaved women and men, these are all oral histories, for a simple reason: As Mary Anderson, age eighty-six, born on a plantation in Wake County, North Carolina, says during her interview, "We were allowed to have prayer meetings in our homes and we also went to the white folks' church. But they would not teach any of us to read and write. Books and papers were forbidden." Writing is power. Enslaved people were intentionally kept powerless. And if they could write down the facts of their lives, the casual violence, the division of families, the lists on which they appeared as property alongside furniture and rugs, what might they say?

The WPA narratives were created to reflect the lives of those humans who were once bought and sold, and in some ways they are a treasure trove of information, filled with the stories of people too often forgotten because of the inclination to paper over incendiary times and truths. "You keeps on asking about me, lady," says Boston Blackwell, age ninety-eight, to a WPA interviewer. "I ain't never been asked about myself in my whole life!"

But reading between the lines, the narratives are a troubling trove as well, as notable for what's missing or massaged into place as they are for what is on the page. Most of the interviewers were white, eliciting stories from men and women, almost all of them living in the American South during the Jim Crow era, who had once been the property of white people. It's instructive to note that most of the narratives are rendered in dialect, *dese* and *dems* and *dose,* except for those done by a small group of Black interviewers. Those accounts were also more likely to include the cruelty of life enslaved, while many of the stories elicited by white interviewers emphasized the kindness of slave owners and the difficulties of life as a free person. If the questions from white interviewers were leading, would it be surprising if the answers from people formerly enslaved were designed to comply, to placate? There's a suspicious sameness to some of the accounts that makes a reader wonder about the template for the questions and the steering of the conversation.

And yet a personality sometimes bursts forth. "They never had enough clothes on to keep a cat warm," W. L. Boast recalls of the men and women sold by speculators. "The women never wore anything but a thin dress and a petticoat and one underwear. I've seen the ice balls hangin' on to the bottom of their dresses as they ran along, just like sheep in a pasture before they are sheared."

And occasionally, though it feels as though the interviews were focused specifically on recollections of the institution of slavery and the aftermath of the Civil War, there are quotidian moments that are as lambent as an oil painting. William L. Dunwoody was ninety-eight and living in Little Rock when he reminisced to Samuel S. Taylor, one of only two Black men doing WPA interviews in Arkansas and considered by some to be perhaps the most able interviewer on the entire project:

Between ten and eleven o'clock, the cook would blow the horn again and the children would come in from play. There would be a large bowl and a large spoon for each group of larger children. There would be enough children in each group to get around the bowl comfortably. One would take a spoon of what was in the bowl and then pass the spoon to his neighbor. His neighbor would take a spoonful and then pass the spoon on, and so on until everyone would have a spoonful. Then they would begin again, and so on until the bowl was empty.

This is history, small-bore but indelible. This is life. If only William Dunwoody had sat down with paper and pen and told it whole, without an interlocutor, even one as skillful as Taylor. I bet he had a book inside him, that man.

It's a bit ironic that some of the most vivid written accounts of actual daily existence, as opposed to dates and treaties, come to us from fiction, not history. Many readers may have learned about whaling from Melville and *Moby-Dick*, the Victorian debtors' prisons from Dickens and *Little Dorrit*. A good novelist knows that sometimes the stuff of everyday life is the bedrock of a book a reader can walk through and live in. But the kind of people who actually live those everyday lives may feel they are not worthy of a story. They are just going to work, making meals, diapering babies, getting by, which is a kind of history but not the kind we've learned to record, to value, to commit to paper.

Some years ago, at the public library in Minneapolis, a woman told me a bit of such a story, her story, the American story. She had fled Somalia as a teenager, lived in a refugee camp, then wound up in the Twin Cities, living in a neighborhood with so many who had come from her native country that it had been nicknamed Little Mogadishu. She'd married another Somali refugee, divorced him, struggled through college, worked as a home health aide, raised two children, and worried about whether they had become so thoroughly American that they would forget their national and religious heritage, and worried that they would not be American enough to satisfy the descendants of Europeans who had settled the state many years before. When asked if she felt more Somali or more American, she replied softly, "May I say both? I would like to say both."

"You should write all this down," I said, and she waved a hand as though she were waving the words away. "I am not a writer like you," she said.

E. L. Doctorow once famously said of writing a novel, "It's like driving a car at night: you never see further than your headlights, but you can make the whole trip that way." The thing is, it sometimes seems as though that is not only true of writing a novel but also of living our lives, living in an indefinite, infinite now. But if we live from headlight to headlight, will we remember what we saw on the road?

It is often said that Americans are poor students of history. Perhaps some of that is because we tend to be push-push people, citizens of a relatively young country, on the move and on the go.

But maybe we would be more engaged in the events of our shared past if they felt more like the events of our personal present.

There is a famous story in my extended family: It is the Depression; my grandfather has many children and little money. On Christmas Eve he drives to the post office, where a tree is displayed over the door, parks in front of it, and climbs onto the roof of the car to take down the tree for his family. A police officer drives up and asks what he is doing. When my grandfather tells him, the police officer helps him take the tree and affix it to the roof of his car. Merry Christmas, and God bless the boys in blue.

This story operates on many levels, beginning with the fact that it is challenging to imagine the rather stout grandfather I knew on the roof of a car. But this happened in the 1930s, and he was younger, and times were tough. It is a story that tells you something about being a father in an era of widespread need, and about community in that era.

There are too few such stories written down, handed down, made part of history alongside the doings of exploration, economics, and government. Relying on that kind of history provides a skewed view of the world because it is almost entirely the history of deeds done by white men, who wrote down what happened as they saw fit, picking and choosing and editing and deleting. And so the rest of us become invisible, at best bit players in the sweep of history.

It is mainly in stories, memories, anecdotes,

everyday experiences, that the true place of women, people of color, immigrants, all those who had no seat at the tables where the big decisions were made, will not only be told but be as central as they actually were in day-to-day life. The French Revolution and Marie Antoinette's oft-invoked (and probably apocryphal) comment about eating cake suddenly takes on a different cast when you understand that one of the revolution's fulcrums was women rioting over grain prices because there was no bread and their children were hungry. Again the historian Arthur Schlesinger, Jr.: "Women have constituted the most spectacular casualty of traditional history. They have made up at least half the human race; but you could never tell that by looking at the books historians write. The forgotten man is nothing to the forgotten woman."

The good news is that Schlesinger made that point in the introduction to a book in which women step into the light largely because they have written down their own stories. In the early twentieth century a champion of women's suffrage living in Topeka, Kansas, named Lilla Day Monroe solicited the personal histories of the women who had settled in that state. More than half a century later, her great-granddaughter Joanna Stratton opened some drawers in the attic of the family home and found those personal memoirs, which she compiled into a book called *Pioneer Women*. While my Somali acquaintance could not be persuaded to write down the particulars of what she believed was a humdrum life, Stratton's great-grandmother had over time convinced eight hundred women that it was important that they do so, although, as one woman said of her mother, they might think, "Oh, there is nothing to be said about me of importance."

If by that she meant that she did not serve in the legislature, found churches or colleges, make large fortunes and open banks, she would be correct. What these women did do was create life, and not just by having the children that they sometimes delivered themselves in dugout homes with dirt floors. Oh, the stories they tell, of fighting fires and drought, of malaria and malnourishment, of coyotes and wolves. There are things that seem plucked right from western movies: saloons, cattle rustling, a plague of grasshoppers. There are picnics, parades, piano playing, weddings, and funerals.

Carrie Stearns Smith recalled how, in 1867, she arrived by stagecoach: "At one point we had forded a stream with a border of brush, and rounding a hill across the ford he [the driver] pointed to a small new grave. Such a sadness possessed me, as I pictured to myself the delay in camp, the suffering of the little one, the absence of medical skill, the death, the burial, and the grief of leaving that freshly heaped mound. But hundreds of such mounds have marked the advance of pioneers."

A woman named Jessie Shepard, who came from New York State to join her parents in 1880, recollected the travails of the early years: "One year cinch bugs took the corn. That was the year we had a bunch of about sixty hogs, doing well too, and after the corn was ruined we could hardly give them away." Anna Biggs illustrated the way in which the newcomers made opportunity from setbacks: "Malaria or ague, as they called it then, was the bane of the early settlers' lives. When Mr. Biggs was so with it that Mrs. Biggs had to cut the wood, she put the baby behind him on the corded bedstead where his shiverings joggled the baby off to sleep."

On a happier note, India Simmons wrote of her mother's handiwork, "Such quilts! Appliqued patterns of flowers and ferns, put on with stitches so dainty as to be almost invisible," as well as "a wool carpet for which she herself had spun and dyed the wool." Catherine Cavender said, "Our joy rides were horseback rides! Wild dashes across the prairie, the wind painting our cheek with nature's red! Western women and girls were expert riders, and one of the best and most graceful riders of the day was Mrs. A. D. Gilkeson. I do not dare tell how the Grandmas of today used to 'cut-up' on horseback—you might suspect that Grandma was not exactly as shy and back-numberish as she would have you believe."

Who was Mrs. A. D. Gilkeson? We do not know, and yet we can see her in our mind's eye, galloping across the prairie, part of a generation of women and girls who worked to create new lives in the Kansas countryside and told us all about it afterward. This is as much a part of history as when the territory joined the union: perhaps more, because it comes alive in a way that a date seldom does, just as the experiences of that Somali woman who refused to write because she did not think of herself as a writer might say more about immigration than laws or statistics.

If, in good times and bad times and ordinary times, people who may not think of themselves as writers begin to set their stories down, in their own voices, in whichever way they choose, it will make history, make it truer, fairer, richer. We need to hear from everyone, durable words, like the letters Sandy wrote to Harry as a war bride, the essays written by the nursing students at Yale, the recollections of those Kansas women making a home amid hardship. We need the words of people whose words were unremarked in histories of the past. If those unaccustomed to the act of everyday writing can find ways to recover that urge to sit down and produce thoughts, musings, letters for their children, their friends, the future, we will not only know what happened during their lifetimes, we will know how it felt. As Anne Frank showed the world, as the Freedom Writers learned themselves, history is our story. Those who write it own it, today and always. Why not you?

ONE NIGHT AT A BOOK SIGNING IN Winnetka, Illinois, a small boy approached my table with a look of mingled disbelief and terror on his face. "She's writing in books! She's writing in books!" he cried as he turned to his mother, obviously having learned young, as did I, that books are sacred objects never to be defaced by pencil or crayon.

But perhaps every never deserves a sometimes, and if there was ever a book in which someone might properly write, it is this one. The invitation has been issued: Tell your story, record your thoughts, note your feelings, write it down.

Here is a place to begin . . .

ABOUT THE AUTHOR

ANNA QUINDLEN is a novelist and journalist whose work has appeared on fiction, nonfiction, and self-help bestseller lists. She is the author of nine novels: *Object Lessons, One True Thing, Black and Blue, Blessings, Rise and Shine, Every Last One, Still Life with Bread Crumbs, Miller's Valley,* and *Alternate Side.* Her memoir *Lots of Candles, Plenty of Cake,* published in 2012, was a #1 *New York Times* bestseller. Her book *A Short Guide to a Happy Life* has sold more than a million copies. While a columnist at *The New York Times* she won the Pulitzer Prize and published two collections, *Living Out Loud* and *Thinking Out Loud.* Her *Newsweek* columns were collected in *Loud and Clear.*

Facebook.com/annaquindlen

Instagram: @annaqwrites

This book was set in Fournier, a typeface named for Pierre-Simon Fournier (1712–68), the youngest son of a French printing family. He started out engraving woodblocks and large capitals, then moved on to fonts of type. In 1736 he began his own foundry and made several important contributions in the field of type design; he is said to have cut 147 alphabets of his own creation. Fournier is probably best remembered as the designer of St. Augustine Ordinaire, a face that served as the model for the Monotype Corporation's Fournier, which was released in 1925.